Stitch Collection
Textured Crochet

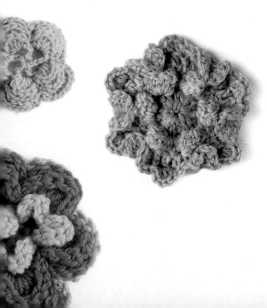

Stitch Collection
Textured Crochet

More than 70 designs with easy-to-follow charts

Helen Jordan

St. Martin's Griffin
New York

www.stmartins.com

Library of Congress Cataloging-in-
Publication Data Available Upon Request

ISBN-10: 0-312-37375-9
ISBN-13: 978-0-312-37375-7

QUAR: CSPT

First published in the United States by
St. Martin's Griffin

Conceived, designed and produced by
Quarto Publishing plc
The Old Brewery
6 Blundell Street
London N7 9BH

Project Editor: Lindsay Kaubi
Art Editor: Julie Joubinaux
Designer: Andrew Easton
Assistant Art Directors: Penny Cobb,
Caroline Guest
Illustrators: Kuo Kang Chen, Coral Mula
Text Editor: Sue Viccars
Pattern Checker: Betty Willett
Photographer: Philip Wilkins
Proofreader: Diana Chambers
Indexer: Helen Snaith

Art Director: Moira Clinch
Publisher: Paul Carslake

Manufactured in Hong Kong by
Modern Age Repro House Ltd
Printed in China by 1010 Printing
International Ltd

First U.S. Edition: September 2007

10 9 8 7 6 5 4 3 2 1

CONTENTS

Crochet is an incredibly versatile and creative activity, and by looking at the patterns in this book you will see just how many fascinating variations in textured effects can be achieved in simple ways. It is my fond hope that you will be encouraged by the techniques in this book to make alterations to familiar patterns and to add your own design elements to your own projects.

The book is organized into nine sections of related techniques, each covering a broad method of achieving a textured crochet surface. Within each section there are several subsections exploring in-depth some of the design possibilities. In each subsection, I have taken an idea and "played" with it, coaxing out all of its variations in order to introduce you to its possibilities.

Some crocheters love working from written instructions, others prefer to work from charted patterns. This book offers the best of both worlds, including both, along with clear color photographs of each stitch design.

I hope you enjoy expanding your crochet vocabulary with the ideas in this book.

Helen Jordan

About this Book

The book begins with Crochet Essentials, where you'll find everything you need to work the stitch patterns in the the book. This is followed by the Stitch Selector, where you can choose the "family" of stitches you'd like to explore. At the heart of the book is the Stitch Collection, a directory of inspiring textured stitch samples divided into nine broad sections.

Crochet Essentials (pages 8–25)
Crochet Essentials will help you learn or revive basic crochet skills. Everything you need to get started is covered along with comprehensive information on stitches and techniques needed to work the designs in the book, all shown in easy-to-follow steps.

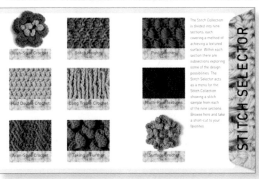

Stitch Selector (pages 26–27)
These pages act as a menu, showing stitch samples from all nine sections of the book. Each section covers a "family" of related techniques. Browse here and take a short cut to your favorites.

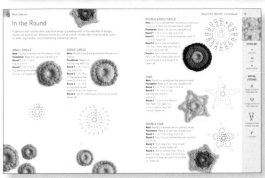

Stitch Collection (pages 28–91)
The Stitch Collection is where you'll find the stitch samples. Photographs clearly show what they look like and written instructions and charted diagrams describe how to work the patterns. The Stitch Key gives a summary of the stitches needed for each section.

Fold-out Flap
Opposite page 95 you'll find a handy fold-out flap featuring an instant reference to the basic stitches, abbreviations, and symbols, which you can leave open as you work through the book.

CROCHET ESSENTIALS

In this section you will find a guide to equipment and materials needed for crochet as well as descriptions of the basic stitches.

Equipment and Materials

To take up crochet, all you need is a crochet hook, a ball of yarn, and few simple accessories.

Hooks

Crochet hooks may be made from aluminum, steel, wood, bamboo, or plastic. They are available in a variety of sizes to suit different types of yarn and to enable you to make your stitches larger or smaller (see Measuring Gauge, page 24).

There appears to be no standardization of hook sizing between manufacturers. The points and throats of different brands of hooks can vary in shape which affects the size of stitch they produce.

Hook sizes are quoted differently in the United States and Europe, and some brands of hooks are labeled with more than one type of numbering. Choosing a hook is largely a matter of personal preference and depends on factors such as hand size, weight of hook, and whether you like the feel of aluminum or plastic in your hand.

The hook sizes quoted in pattern instructions are a useful guide, but you may find that you need to use smaller or larger hook sizes, depending on the brand, to achieve the correct gauge for a pattern.

Crochet hooks are produced in a range of materials.

Comparative crochet hook sizes (from smallest to largest)					
Steel			Aluminum or Plastic		
US	UK	Metric (mm)	US	UK	Metric (mm)
14	6	0.60		14	2.00
13	5½			13	
12	5	0.75	B	12	2.50
11	4½		C	11	3.00
10	4	1.00	D	10	
9	3½		E	9	3.50
8	3	1.25	F	8	4.00
7	2½	1.50	G	7	4.50
6	2	1.75	H	6	5.00
5	1½		I	5	5.50
4	1	2.00	J	4	6.00
3	1/0		K	2	7.00
2	2/0	2.50			
1	3/0	3.00			
0					
00		3.50			

Yarns

There is a huge range of yarns available to use for crochet, from very fine cotton to chunky wool; however, as a general rule, the easiest yarns to use for textured crochet have a smooth surface and a medium or tight twist. Heavily textured yarns tend to hide the complexity and details of stitch texture, so in general, it is recommended that you use smooth yarns for the textured crochet stitches featured in this book.

Yarns are available in acrylic, pure wool, and cotton blends.

Accessories

Only a few accessories are needed to complete a crochet project.

1 Small, sharp, pointed scissors for trimming yarn.

2 A tape measure that shows both inches and centimeters on the same side for checking your gauge (see page 24).

3 To hold your work during assembly, choose pins with large heads that will not disappear between the stitches.

4 Yarn needles are the best type to use for sewing seams. They have a large eye and a blunt tip that will not split the yarn, and are available in a range of sizes.

Getting Started

Holding the Hook

The hook is held in the right hand (if you are right-handed). There are two ways to hold a crochet hook: like a pencil (a) or like a knife (b). The hook should face downward.

A   B

Making a Slip Knot

Almost every piece of crochet begins with a slip knot.

STEP 1
Loop the yarn in the direction shown, insert the hook through the loop to catch the yarn leading to the ball (not the short tail), and pull it through to make a loop.

STEP 2
Pull gently on both yarn ends to tighten the knot against the hook.

Alternative Slip Knot

To work a number of stitches into a slip knot, you may need to make the slip knot so that it slides up from the tail end of the yarn rather than the ball. To do this, place the yarn ball at the left and the tail at the right as shown in the diagram.

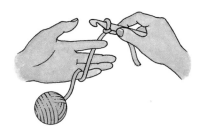

Holding the Yarn

The left hand (if you are right-handed) controls the supply of yarn. It is important to maintain an even tension on the yarn. One method is to wind the yarn around your fingers, as shown below.

To form a stitch use your first finger to bring the yarn into position so it may be caught by the hook and pulled through to make a new loop. Note the direction of the yarn around the tip of the hook.

Basic Stitches

Chain Stitch (ch)

Most pieces of crochet begin with a foundation chain of a certain number of stitches. Chains worked at the beginning of a row, or as part of a stitch pattern, are worked in the same way as below.

STEP 1

Hold the yarn and slip knot as shown on page 10. Wrap the yarn around the hook in the direction shown (or catch it with the hook).

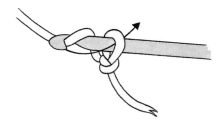

STEP 2

Pull a new loop through the loop on the hook. 1 ch made.

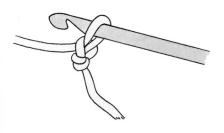

STEP 3

Repeat steps 1 and 2 as required, moving your left hand every few stitches to hold the chain just below the hook.

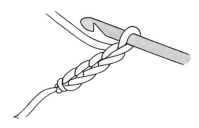

Slip Stitch (sl st)

STEP 1

Begin with a length of chains. Insert the hook in the second chain from the hook, wrap the yarn around the hook, and pull a new loop through both the work and the loop on the hook. 1 sl st made.

STEP 2

Repeat step 1 in each chain to the end. 1 row of sl st made.

Single Crochet (sc)

STEP 1

Begin with a length of chains. Insert the hook in the second chain from the hook, wrap the yarn around the hook, and pull the new loop through the chain only.

STEP 2

Wrap the yarn around the hook, and pull a loop through both loops on the hook.

STEP 3

One loop remains on the hook. 1 sc made. Repeat steps 1 and 2 in each chain to the end. 1 row of sc made.

Half Double Crochet (hdc)

STEP 1

Begin with a length of chains. Wrap the yarn around the hook, and insert the hook in the third chain from the hook.

STEP 2

Pull a loop through this chain. You now have three loops on the hook. Wrap the yarn around the hook again. Pull through all three loops on the hook.

STEP 3

One loop remains on the hook. 1 hdc made. Repeat steps 1 through 3 in each chain to the end. 1 row of hdc made.

Double Crochet (dc)

STEP 1

Begin with a length of chains. Wrap the yarn around the hook, and insert the hook in the fourth chain from the hook.

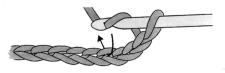

STEP 2

Pull a loop through this chain to make three loops on the hook. Wrap the yarn around the hook again. Pull a new loop through the first two loops on the hook. Two loops remain on the hook. Wrap the yarn around the hook again. Pull a new loop through both loops on the hook.

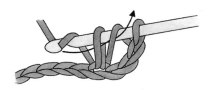

STEP 3

1 dc made. Repeat steps 1 through 3 in each chain to the end. 1 row of dc made.

Extended Double Crochet (edc)

STEP 1

Begin with a length of chains. Wrap the yarn around the hook, and insert the hook in the fourth chain from the hook.

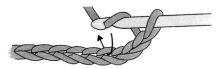

STEP 2

Pull a loop through this chain; three loops on the hook. Wrap the yarn around the hook again. Pull a new loop through only the first loop on the hook; three loops remain on the hook. Wrap the yarn around the hook again. Pull a new loop through the first two loops on the hook; two loops remain on the hook. Wrap the yarn around the hook again. Pull a new loop through both loops on the hook.

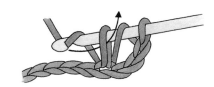

STEP 3

1 edc made. Repeat steps 1 through 2 in each chain to the end. 1 row of edc made.

Treble Crochet (tr)

STEP 1

Begin with a length of chains. Wrap the yarn twice around the hook, and insert the hook in the fifth chain from the hook.

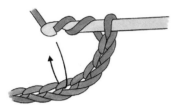

STEP 2

Pull a loop through this chain. You now have four loops on the hook. Wrap the yarn again and pull through the first two loops.

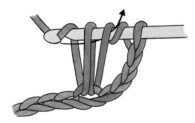

STEP 3

Three loops remain on the hook. Wrap the yarn around the hook and pull through the first two loops.

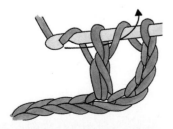

STEP 4

Two loops remain on the hook. Wrap the yarn again and pull through the two remaining loops.

STEP 5

1 tr made. Repeat steps 1 through 5 in each chain to the end. 1 row of tr made.

NOTE

Extended treble crochets can be worked in a similar way to extended double crochets (see page 13). It is the stage where the yarn is pulled through one loop only that makes it an extended stitch.

Basic Techniques

Working in Rows

When you work the first row into the foundation chain, you begin the first stitch in the second, third, fourth, or fifth chain from the hook, depending on the height of the stitch you are making; the one, two, three, or four chains that you skip stand instead of the first stitch of the first row. Every following row begins with a similar number of chains, called the turning chain(s). The next examples show rows of doubles, with three turning chains.

More complicated stitch patterns usually follow the same principle.

Turning the Work

STEP 1

When the first row is complete, turn the work. You can turn it either clockwise or counterclockwise, but a neater edge will result if you turn the work away from you.

At the beginning of the next row, work a number of turning chains to correspond with the stitch in use, as listed in the table, right. These chains will stand for the first stitch of the new row, and are counted as one stitch. Exceptions to this rule are stated in the individual instructions.

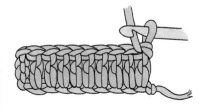

TABLE OF TURNING CHAINS

single crochet	1 chain
extended single crochet	2 chains
half double	2 chains
double	3 chains
treble	4 chains
double treble	5 chains

Note: These are the usual numbers of turning chains used for the basic stitches. Sometimes two chains are needed for single crochet, and the requirements of more complicated stitch patterns may vary.

STEP 2

Work the appropriate number of chains (three are shown here). Skip the last stitch of the previous row and work into the next stitch. The hook is normally inserted under the top two threads of each stitch, as shown. (When the hook is to be inserted elsewhere, pattern instructions will indicate this.)

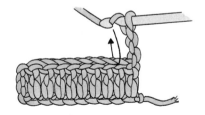

TIP

The turning chain usually replaces the first stitch of the new row. The instructions and patterns will tell you if this is not the case.

Continues on page 16

STEP 3

At the end of the row, work the last stitch into the top of the chains at the beginning of the previous row. Then repeat steps 1 through 3.

Insert the hook as required, wrap the yarn over it, and pull a loop through. Leave a tail of about 4 in. (10cm). Work one chain, and continue the pattern. If you are using a solid stitch work the next few stitches for about 2 in. (5 cm) enclosing the yarn tail, then pull gently on the tail and snip off the excess.

Changing Colors

Use this method for a neat join between colors. The first ball need not be fastened off: it may be left aside for a few rows or stitches in the course of a multicolored pattern.

Fastening Off

To fasten off the yarn securely, work one chain, then cut the yarn at least 4 in. (10cm) away from the work, and pull the tail through the loop on the hook, tightening it gently.

STEP 1

Work up to the final "yrh, pull through" of the last stitch in the old color and wrap the new color around the hook.

STEP 2

Use the new color to complete the stitch.

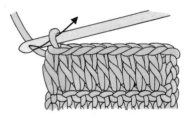

Joining in a New Yarn

Sometimes yarn is fastened off in one position and then rejoined elsewhere (to work an edging, for example). Also, if your first ball of yarn runs out, you will have to join in another.

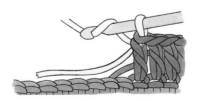

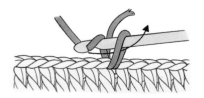

STEP 3

Continue in the new color.

Working in Rounds

Crochet may be worked in rounds instead of rows. If a flat circle is required, it is necessary to increase the number of stitches on every round. If the increases are grouped together to make corners, then a triangle, square, hexagon, or other flat shape will result. If no increasing is worked, the crochet will form a tube.

Chain Ring

This is one way to begin when working in rounds. The chain ring may be any size, as required, leaving a small or large hole at the center of the work.

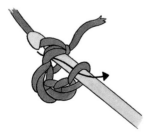

Make the number of chains required. Without twisting the chains, join them into a ring with a slip stitch into the first chain made.

Work a Round

STEP 1

Each round usually begins with a number of turning chains, to stand for the first stitch. Here, three turning chains stand for the first double. The first round is usually worked by inserting the hook in the center of the chain ring.

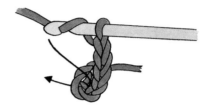

STEP 2

To join the round at the end, work a slip stitch into the last starting chain made. On the following rounds, insert the hook in the normal way under two threads at the top of each stitch, unless directed otherwise

NOTE

Some patterns ask you to turn the work at the end of each round, some do not. Follow the instructions given to achieve the desired result.

Closed Centers

For a round with a closed center, work the slip knot so that it pulls up from the "tail" end rather than the "ball" end (see page 10). Work the number of chains stated in the pattern and then work the required number of stitches in the first chain made. When you have finished the first round, gently pull on the "tail" end of the yarn to close the center. The end will need to be securely stitched into the work. This can be done straight away or when the work is finished.

Fastening Off Rounds

STEP 1

To fasten off when working in rounds, work the slip stitch joining the last round, then cut the yarn leaving a short tail, and draw the tail through the slip stitch.

STEP 2

Reinsert the hook from the back, in the position where the slip stitch was worked, catch the yarn tail, and pull it through to the back of the work.

Stitch Variations

Basic stitches may be varied in many ways, for example, by working several stitches in the same place, by inserting the hook in a different place, by working several stitches together, or by working in the reverse direction. In surface crochet, chain stitches are overlaid onto a crochet background or taller stitches are worked into an existing fabric.

Working Several Stitches in the Same Place

Increasing

This technique is used to increase the total number of stitches when shaping a garment or other item. Increases may be worked at the edges of flat pieces, or at any point along a row or round.

Patterning

Two, three, or more stitches may be worked into the same place to make a fan of stitches, often called a shell. The total number of stitches is increased, so when working a stitch pattern other stitches are worked together or skipped to compensate.

Working into One Loop

Here, five doubles are shown worked into the same foundation chain, making a shell. If the hook is inserted under just one loop at the top of a stitch, the empty loop creates a ridge on either the front or the back of the fabric.

Front Loop Only

If the hook is inserted under the front loop only, the empty back loop will show as a ridge on the other side of the work.

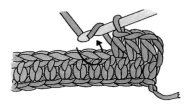

Back Loop Only

If the hook is inserted under the back loop only, the empty front loop creates a ridge on the side of the work facing you. This example shows single crochet.

Note: In this book, "front loop" means the loop nearest to you, at the top of the stitch, and "back loop" means the farther loop, whether you are working a right-side or a wrong-side row.

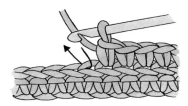

Middle Loop Only

When a row of half doubles has been worked, there are three loops at the top of the stitch instead of the usual two. Insert the hook under the middle loop only to create a single horizontal thread across the stitch on both sides of the work.

Into a Chain Space

The hook is inserted into the space below one or more chains. Here, a double is being worked into a one chain space.

Post Stitches

These are created by inserting the hook around the stem of the stitch below, from the front or the back. These two examples show post doubles, but shorter or longer stitches may be worked in a similar way:

Front Post Double (FPdc)

STEP 1

Wrap the yarn around the hook, insert the hook from the front to the back at right of the next stitch, and bring it out at left of the same stitch. The hook is now round the stem of the stitch.

STEP 2

Complete the double in the usual way. A ridge forms on the other side of the work.

Back Post Double (BPdc)

STEP 1

Wrap the yarn around the hook, insert the hook from the back through to the front at right of the next stitch, and through to the back again at left of the same stitch.

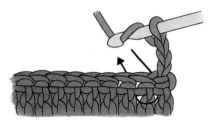

STEP 2

Complete the double in the usual way. A ridge forms on the side of the work facing you.

Working Several Stitches Together

Decreasing

Two or more stitches may be joined together at the top to decrease the total number of stitches when shaping the work, using the same method as for clusters, below.

Patterning

Joining groups of stitches together makes several decorative stitch formations: clusters, puffs, bobbles, and popcorns.

Cluster

A cluster is a group of stitches, joined closely together at the top. (Sometimes the term is also used for groups joined at both top and bottom.)

STEP 1

Work each of the stitches to be joined up to the last "yrh, pull through" that will complete it. One loop from each stitch to be joined should remain on the hook, plus the loop from the previous stitch. Wrap the yarn around the hook once again.

STEP 2

Pull a loop through all the loops on the hook. One loop now remains on the hook. Three doubles are shown here worked together, but any number of any type of stitch may be worked together in a similar way.

Puff

A puff is normally a group of three or more half doubles, joined at both top and bottom (a three-half-double puff is shown below).

STEP 1

* Wrap the yarn around the hook, insert the hook where required, draw through a loop, repeat from * two (or more) times in the same place. You now have seven loops (or more) on the hook. Wrap the yarn round the hook again, and pull through all the loops on the hook.

STEP 2

Often, one chain is worked to close the puff.

Bobble

A bobble is usually a group of several doubles (or longer stitches) joined at both top and bottom. It is often surrounded by shorter stitches, and worked on a wrong-side row (a three-double bobble is shown here).

STEP 1

* Wrap the yarn around the hook, insert the hook where required, pull a loop through, wrap the yarn around the hook, pull through the first two loops, repeat from * two (or more) times in the same place. Wrap the yarn around the hook, and pull through all loops.

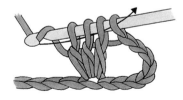

STEP 2

Work one chain to close.

Popcorn

A popcorn is formed when several complete doubles (or longer stitches) are worked in the same place, and the top of the first stitch is joined to the last to make a "cup" shape. A four-double popcorn is shown below.

STEP 1
Work four doubles (or number required) in the same place.

STEP 2
Slip the last loop off the hook. Reinsert the hook in the top of the first double of the group, as shown, and catch the empty loop. (On a wrong-side row, reinsert the hook from the back, to push the popcorn to the right side of the work.)

STEP 3
Pull this loop through to close the top of the popcorn.

TIP

Sometimes the closing stitch of a popcorn is worked through the back loop only of the first stitch of the group and sometimes through the stitch made just before the group.

Picot

Formed by three or more chains closed into a ring with a slip stitch (or a single crochet).

STEP 1
Work three chains (or number required). Insert the hook as instructed. The arrow shows how to insert the hook down through the top of the previous single crochet.

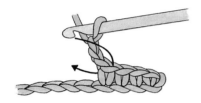

STEP 2
Wrap the yarn around the hook and pull through all the loops to close the picot with a slipstitch.

Crab Stitch

Usually used as an edging and worked from left to right, giving an extra twist to each stitch.

STEP 1
After completing a right-side row, do not turn the work. Insert the hook in the first stitch to the right, turning the hook downward to catch the yarn and pull it through.

STEP 2
Catch the yarn again, and pull it through both loops on the hook to complete the stitch. Repeat steps 1 and 2 to the right.

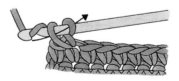

Measuring Gauge

Most crochet patterns recommend a "gauge." This is the number of stitches (or pattern repeats) and rows to a given measurement (usually 4 in. or 10cm). For your work to be the correct size, you must match this gauge as closely as possible. To work out a design of your own, you need to measure your gauge to calculate the stitches and rows required.

The hook size recommended by any pattern or ball band is only a suggestion. Gauge depends not only on the hook and yarn but also on personal technique.

STEP 1

Work a piece of crochet about 6 in. (15cm) square, using the hook, yarn, and stitch pattern required. Press if this is recommended on the ball band. Lay the sample flat and place two pins 4 in. (10cm) apart along the same row, near the center. Count the stitches (or pattern repeats) between them

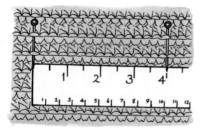

STEP 2

Place two pins 4 in. (10cm) apart on a vertical pattern line near the center, and count the number of rows between them.

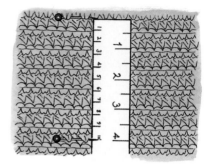

If you have too many stitches (or pattern repeats) or rows to 4 in. (10cm), your work is too tight; repeat the process with another sample made with a larger hook. If you have too few stitches (or pattern repeats), or rows, your work is too loose; try a smaller hook. It is usually more important to match the number of stitches exactly, rather than the number of rows.

Blocking Crochet

Crochet often needs to be blocked before assembly, to "set" the stitches and give a professional finish. Textured crochet requires different blocking techniques from most smooth crochet fabrics. It would be very easy to block away the vast majority of three-dimensional effects you have achieved because you have used the wrong blocking technique.

Crochet Aftercare

It is a good idea to keep a ball band from each project you complete as a reference for washing instructions. Crochet items are best washed gently by hand and dried flat, to keep their shape. Crochet garments should not be hung on coat hangers, but folded and stored flat, away from dust, damp, heat, and sunlight. Clean tissue paper is better than a plastic bag.

STEP 1

Check the ball band to make sure that the yarn will tolerate being wetted. If it will not, avoid blocking the piece by any method.

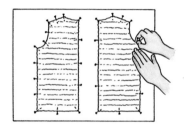

STEP 2

Pin each piece of crochet right side up onto a well-padded surface. With rows straight, pin the pieces in place inserting pins evenly all around at right angles to the edges. If necessary, gently ease the pieces to size, checking measurements as you go. Spray lightly with clean cold water and leave until thoroughly dry before unpinning.

TIP

Textured crochet usually needs less blocking than other crochet techniques. Be gentle so as to avoid spoiling the textured effects you have achieved.

Shade and dye lot numbers

Weight and length of yarn ball

Washing and pressing instructions

Fiber content of yarn

Irish-style Crochet
28–33

Stitch Heights
34–43

Half Double Crochet
54–59

Long Treble Crochet
60–67

Aran-style Crochet
74–77

Taking it Further
78–87

Post Stitches
44–53

Multi-row Textures
68–73

Surface Crochet
88–91

The Stitch Collection is divided into nine sections, each covering a method of achieving a textured surface. Within each section there are subsections exploring some of the design possibilities. The Stitch Selector acts as a menu for the Stitch Collection showing a stitch sample from each of the nine sections. Browse here and take a short-cut to your favorites.

STITCH SELECTOR

IRISH-STYLE CROCHET

Irish crochet is traditionally worked in very fine white cotton thread; however, in this section you will find worsted weight wool variations of these amazing motifs.

Leaves

When working the leaves, use only the back loop of the stitches made on the previous row to achieve the textured effect. Using only the front loop produces a much flatter, more subtle effect.

BASIC LEAF

Foundation: Make 10 ch.
Row 1: Skip 1 ch, 1 sc in 1 loop only of ea of next 8 ch, 3 sc in last ch, 1 sc in 1 loop only of ea ch along other side of foundation ch, turn.
Row 2: 1 ch, skip first st, 1 sc in back loop only of next 9 sc, 3 sc in back loop only of sc at end, 1 sc in back loop only of next 9 sc, turn.
Rows 3–5: Rep row 2 three times. Fasten off.

STEPPED LEAF

Foundation: Make 10 ch.
Row 1: Skip 1 ch, 1 sc in 1 loop only of ea of next 8 ch, 3 sc in last ch, 1 sc in 1 loop only of ea ch along other side of foundation ch, turn.

Row 2: 1 ch, skip first st, 1 sc in back loop only of ea of next 9 sc, 3 sc in back loop only of sc at end, 1 sc in back loop only of ea of next 7 sc, turn.
Row 3: 1 ch, skip first st, 1 sc in back loop only of ea of next 7 sc, 3 sc in back loop only of sc at end, 1 sc in back loop only of ea of next 7 sc, turn.
Row 4: 1 ch, skip first st, 1 sc in back loop only of ea of next 7 sc, 3 sc in back loop only of sc at end, 1 sc in back loop only of ea of next 5 sc, turn.
Row 5: 1 ch, skip first st, 1 sc in back loop only of ea of next 5 sc, 3 sc in back loop only of sc at end, 1 sc in back loop only of ea of next 5 sc. Fasten off.

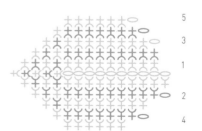

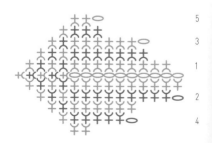

POINTED LEAF

Foundation: Make 10 ch.

Row 1: Skip 1 ch, 1 sc in 1 loop only of ea of next 8 ch, 5 sc in last ch, 1 sc in 1 loop only of ea ch along other side of foundation ch, turn.

Row 2: 1 ch, skip first st, 1 sc in back loop only of next 10 sc, 5 sc in back loop only of sc at end, 1 sc in back loop only of next 10 sc, turn.

Row 3: 1 ch, skip first st, 1 sc in back loop only of next 11 sc, 5 sc in back loop only of sc at end, 1 sc in back loop only of next 11 sc. Fasten off.

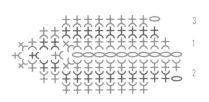

STITCH KEY

slip stitch

chain

SPECIAL STITCHES

single crochet in back loop only

2 single crochets in back loop only

3 single crochets in back loop only

3 single crochets together into back loops only (sc3tog)

HEAVILY RIDGED LEAF

This design is worked following the instructions for the basic leaf, but with the addition of a padding cord, another traditional Irish crochet technique. Cut a long length of the yarn you will be using, fold it in two, and work the sc over this as well as into the crochet fabric.

RIDGED CHEVRON FABRIC

Motifs are not the only possibility using this technique; here is a fabric idea for you to try.

Foundation: Make a multiple of 10 ch, plus 2. From row 2 work in the back loop only.

Row 1: Skip first ch, 1 sc in second ch from hook, *1 sc in ea of next 3 ch, sc3tog, 1 sc in ea of next 3 ch, 3 sc in next st, rep from * to end, omitting 1 sc at end of final rep, turn.

Row 2: 1 ch, 1 sc in same sc, *1 sc in back loop only of next 3 sc, sc3tog in back loop only, 1 sc in back loop only of next 3 sc, 3 sc in back loop only of next st, rep from * to end, omitting 1 sc at end of final rep, turn.

Row 3: Rep row 2 for the length required.

Roses

The rose is a traditional Irish crochet motif. Worked in worsted weight yarn, the motif can be used in all sorts of ways: as a brooch; to decorate shoes; you could even link a number of them together to form a belt or bag handle. Be careful that you don't make the flower so heavy that it distorts any base fabric that it is worked into.

TRADITIONAL ROSE

Foundation: 4 ch, join with sl st into first ch.
Round 1: 1 ch, 6 sc into ring , sl st to ch.
Round 2: 6 ch, (1 dc, 3 ch) 5 times, sl st into 3rd of 6 ch.
Round 3: (1 sc, 1 hdc, 3 dc, 1 hdc, 1 sc in 3-ch loop, sl st in next st) 6 times.
Round 4: (4 ch, sl st in next sl st) 6 times.
Round 5: (1 sc, 1 hdc, 5 dc, 1 hdc, 1 sc in 4-ch loop, sl st in next st) 6 times.
Round 6: (5 ch, sl st in next sl st) 6 times.
Round 7: (1 sc, 1 hdc, 7 dc, 1 hdc, 1 sc in 5-ch loop, sl st in next st) 6 times. Fasten off.

TINY ROSE

Round 1: 3 ch, 6 hdc in first ch, sl st to top of ch.
Round 2: (sl st in front loop only of next hdc, 2 ch) 6 times, sl st in next sl st.
Round 3: 3 sc in each 2-ch loop, sl st in first sc of round.
Round 4: (sl st in middle loop of next hdc, 3 ch) 6 times, sl st in next sl st.
Round 5: (1 sc, 1 hdc, 1 dc, 1 hdc, 1 sc in 3-ch loop, sl st in next st) 6 times.
Round 6: (sl st in back loop of next hdc, 4 ch) 6 times, sl st in next sl st.
Round 7: (1 sc, 1 hdc, 3 dc, 1hdc, 1 sc in 4-ch loop, sl st in next st) 6 times. Fasten off.

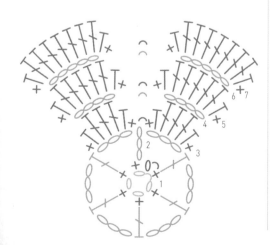

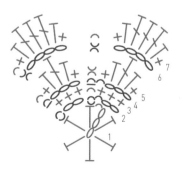

FIVE-PETALED ROSE

Work as for traditional rose, but with only five petals and omitting round 1, so you place dc round 2 of the instructions into the ring.

STITCH KEY

⌒
slip stitch

◯
chain

+
single crochet

T
half double crochet

Ŧ
double crochet

SEVEN-PETALED ROSE

Work as for traditional rose, but with seven petals.

SPECIAL STITCHES

◡
slip stitch in front loop only

◠
slip stitch in middle loop only

⌢
slip stitch in back loop only

SINGLE ROSE

Work first 3 rounds as for five-petaled rose. On round 4, instead of a sl st, work a back post sl st around the stem of the dc.

TWO-COLOR ROSE

Work a six-petaled version of the single rose, using a contrast color for round 5 only.

WATER LILY

Based on the two-color rose, work foundation ring and rounds 1 and 2 in yellow, rounds 3–6 in orange, and round 7 in green. Also, on rounds 5 and 7 change the center stitches to tr, i.e. in round 5, the stitches in the loop become, 1 sc, 1 hdc, 1 dc, 3 tr, 1 dc, 1 hdc, 1 sc. The pattern is similar for round 7.

In the Round

Traditional Irish crochet often uses thick wraps of padding cord. In this selection of designs, rounds are worked over previous rounds to build up a thick, chunky effect that would be useful for belts, bag handles, and embellishing substantial fabrics.

SMALL CIRCLE

Note: Round 2 is worked over the previous round.
Foundation: Make 6 ch, join into ring with sl st.
Round 1: 1 ch, 11 sc in ring, sl st in ch.
Round 2: 1 ch, 15 sc in ring (working over round 1), sl st in ch. Fasten off.

EDGED CIRCLE

Note: Rounds 2 and 3 are worked over the previous rounds.
Foundation: Make 6 ch, join into ring with sl st.
Round 1: 1 ch, 11 sc in ring, sl st in ch.
Round 2: 1 ch, 15 sc in ring (working over round 1), sl st in ch.
Round 3: 1 ch, 19 sc in ring (working over round 2), sl st in ch. Fasten off.
Round 4: Join in contrast yarn, cr st in ea sc to end. Fasten off.

DOUBLE EDGED CIRCLE

Note: Round 2 is worked over the previous round and round 4 is worked into the back loop of round 2.
Foundation: Make 6 ch, join into ring with sl st.
Round 1: 1 ch, 11 sc in ring, sl st in ch.
Round 2: 1 ch, 15 sc in ring (working over round 1), sl st in ch. Fasten off.
Round 3: Join in first contrast yarn, 1 ch, 2 sc in front loop only of ea sc, sl st to 1 ch. Fasten off.
Round 4: Join in second contrast yarn, 2 ch, 2 dc in back loop only of ea sc in round 2, sl st to top of ch. Fasten off.

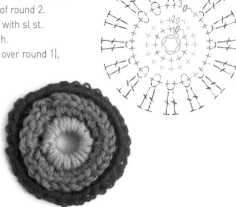

STITCH KEY

⌒
slip stitch

○
chain

✕
single crochet

𝆑
double crochet

SPECIAL STITCHES

single crochet in front loop only

2 single crochets in front loop only

⋎
2 double crochets in back loop only

crab stitch

STAR

Note: Round 2 is worked over the previous round.
Foundation: Make 6 ch, join into ring with sl st.
Round 1: 1 ch, 11 sc in ring, sl st in ch.
Round 2: 1 ch, 15 sc in ring (working over round 1), sl st in ch.
Round 3: * 6 ch, sl st in third ch from hook, 3 ch, skip 2 sc, 1 sl st in next sc, rep from * to end. Fasten off.

DOUBLE STAR

Note: Round 2 is worked over the previous round.
Foundation: Make 6 ch, join into ring with sl st.
Round 1: 1 ch, 11 sc in ring, sl st in ch.
Round 2: 1 ch, 15 sc in ring (working over round 1), sl st in ch.
Round 3: *5 ch, skip 2 sc, 1 sl st in next sc, rep from * to end. Fasten off.
Round 4: Join in contrast color, *3 sc in next 5-ch loop, 3 ch, sl st in first ch, 3 sc in same 5-ch loop, rep from * sl st to first sc. Fasten off.

STITCH HEIGHTS

One of the joys of crochet is the tremendous variety of stitch heights that can be achieved. Using a mixture of stitches, you can create an exciting array of textured designs.

Knot Stitches

Knot stitches use a single long stitch between short stitches. The rows containing the long stitches are alternated with plain single crochet rows to give a subtle overall texture. These stitches are suitable for most garments, accessories, and home accents, as the low profile of the stitches is not vulnerable to damage in use.

ALIGNED KNOT STITCH

Foundation: Make an odd number of chains.
Row 1: sc in second ch from hook, sc in each ch to end, turn.
Row 2: 1 ch, sc in next sc, *tr in next sc, sc in next sc, rep from * to last st, sc in top of tch.
Row 3: 1 ch, sc in each st to end, turn.
Rep rows 2 and 3 for required length, end with row 3.

OFF-SET KNOT STITCH

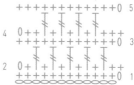

Foundation: Make an odd number of chains.
Row 1: sc in second ch from hook, sc in each ch to end, turn.
Row 2: 1 ch, sc in next sc, *tr in next sc, sc in next sc, rep from * to last st, sc in top of turning ch.
Row 3: 1 ch, sc in each st to end, turn.
Row 4: 1 ch, sc in next 2 sc, *tr in next sc, sc in next sc, rep from * to last 2 sts, sc in next sc, sc in top of tch, turn.
Row 5: 1 ch, sc in each st to end, turn.
Rep rows 2–5 for required length, end with row 5.

TWO-COLORED KNOT STITCH

Work as for Off-set Knot Stitch but change color on each row, keeping all sc rows in the same "background" color.

STRIPED KNOT STITCH (1)

Work as for Off-set Knot Stitch but change color after each sc row for an attractive stripe pattern

chain

STRIPED KNOT STITCH (2)

single crochet

Work as for Off-set Knot Stitch but change color after each row containing tr for another subtle variation on the same theme as Striped Knot Stitch (1).

treble crochet

CONTRAST KNOT STITCH

Work as for Off-set Knot Stitch but change color on rows containing tr, along the row, so that every long stitch is worked in the contrasting color.

CLOSE KNOT STITCH

Work as for Off-set Knot Stitch but after row 1, do not work any more plain sc rows, until the final row, i.e. work row 2, fasten off, do not turn work. Join in yarn at beginning of row, complete as for row 4, fasten off. Rep last two rows to end. Turn, work 1 row sc to finish.

Bobbles

Working a number of stitches into a single stitch in a plain fabric produces a textured surface. These designs explore some of the possibilities on a variety of backgrounds.

MOSSY BOBBLES

Foundation: Make a multiple of 3 ch.
Row 1: 1 sc in second ch from hook, 1 sc in ea ch to end, turn.
Row 2: 1 ch, *(1 dc, 1 tr, 1 dtr) in next st, 2 sc, rep from * to end, omitting 1 sc from end of last rep, turn.
Row 3: 1 ch, *1 sc in dtr, skip 2 sts, 2 sc, rep from * to end, omitting 1 sc from end of last rep, turn.
Row 4: 1 ch, 1 sc in ea st to end, turn.
Row 5: Rep row 4.
Rep rows 2–5 for required length, ending with an sc row.

MULTI-COLOR BOBBLES

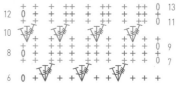

Note: Work the mossy bobble pattern and then follow rows 6–13 below. Change color along the row for bobbles in contrast yarn.
Row 6: 1 ch, 1 sc, *(1 dc, 1 tr, 1 dtr) in next st, 2 sc, rep from * to last st, (1 dc, 1 tr, 1 dtr) in last st, turn.
Row 7: 1 ch, *skip 2 sts, 2 sc, 1 sc in dtr, rep from * to last 2 sts, 2 sc, turn.
Rows 8–9: Rep row 4.
Row 10: 3 ch, (1 tr, 1 dtr) in same st, *2 sc, (1 dc, 1 tr, 1 dtr) in next st, rep from * to last 2 sts, 2 sc, turn.
Row 11: 1 ch, 1 sc, *1 sc in dtr, skip 2 sts, 2 sc, rep from * to last bobble, 1 sc in last st, turn.
Rows 12–13: Rep row 4.
Rep rows 2–13 for required length, ending with an sc row.

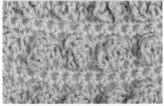

ICE CREAM BOBBLES

Work as for Mossy Bobbles, but change the bobbles to 1 dtr, 1 tr, 1 dc.

RASPBERRY BOBBLES

Work as for Mossy Bobbles, but on the first sc row, work the sc in the dc, instead of the dtr.

STITCH KEY

chain

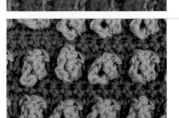

BUBBLEGUM BOBBLES

Work as for Ice Cream Bobbles, but on the first sc row, work the sc in the dc, instead of the dtr.

single crochet

double crochet

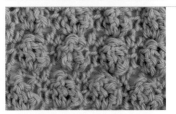

LILAC BOBBLES

Work Mossy Bobbles on a background of hdc, with only 1 row of half doubles between the bobble rows.

treble crochet

double treble crochet

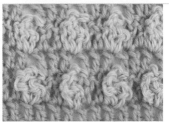

PEACH BOBBLES

Work Mossy Bobbles on a background of dc, with only 1 row of doubles between the bobble rows.

1 double, 1 treble, 1 double treble in same stitch

Ripples

Graduated stitches in a background of short stitches create a variety of textured effects.

GENTLE RIPPLES

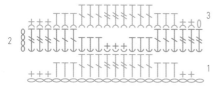

Foundation: Make a multiple of 18 ch + 3.
Row 1: 1 sc in second ch from hook, 1 sc, *3 hdc, 3 dc, 3 tr, 3 dc, 3 hdc, 3 sc, rep from * to end, turn.
Row 2: Working in front loop only, 4 ch, 2 tr, *3 dc, 3 hdc, 3 sc, 3 hdc, 3 dc, 3 tr, rep from * to end, turn.
Row 3: Working in back loop only, 1 ch, 2 sc, *3 hdc, 3 dc, 3 tr, 3 dc, 3 hdc, 3 sc, rep from * to end, turn.
Rep rows 2–3 for required length.

WAVY RIPPLES

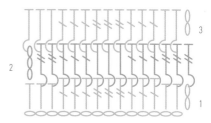

Foundation: Make a multiple of 12 ch + 4.
Row 1: 1 hdc in third ch from hook, 1 hdc, *3 dc, 3 tr, 3 dc, 3 hdc, rep from * to end, turn.
Row 2: 3 ch, 2 FPtr, *3 FPdc, 3 FPhdc, 3 FPdc, 3 FPtr, rep from * to end, turn.
Row 3: 2 ch, 2 BPhdc, *3 BPdc, 3 BPtr, 3 BPdc, 3 BPhdc, rep from * to end, turn.
Rep rows 2–3 for required length.

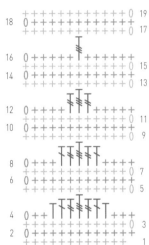

STYLIZED RIPPLES

Note: Change color along row to work the taller stitches only in the contrast yarn.

Foundation: Make a multiple of 10 ch + 3.

Row 1: 1 sc in second ch from hook, 1 sc in ea ch to end, turn.

Row 2: 1 ch, 1 sc in ea st to end, turn.

Row 3: Rep row 2.

Row 4: 1 ch, 2 sc, *1 hdc, 1 dc, 1 tr, 1 dtr, 1 tr, 1 dc, 1 hdc, 3 sc, rep from * to end, turn.

Rows 5 –7: Rep row 2.

Row 8: 1 ch, 3 sc, *1 dc, 1 tr, 1 dtr, 1 tr, 1 dc, 5 sc, rep from * to end, omitting 1 sc from end of final rep, turn.

Rows 9–11: Rep row 2.

Row 12: 1 ch, 4 sc, *1 tr, 1 dtr, 1 tr, 7 sc, rep from * to end, omitting 1 sc from end of final rep, turn.

Rows 13–15: Rep row 2.

Row 16: 1 ch, 5 sc, *1 dtr, 9 sc, rep from * to end, turn.

Rows 17–19: Rep row 2. Fasten off.

STITCH KEY

For basic stitch symbols, see flap opposite page 95

SPECIAL STITCHES

single/half double/double/treble crochets in front loop only

single/half double/double/treble crochets in back loop only

front post half double/double/treble crochets

back post half double/double/treble crochets

Wedges

The designs in this section take one simple method of using different stitch heights as post stitches and play with it in a number of ways—there are other ways, but these should get you started!

WEDGE—LONG TO SHORT

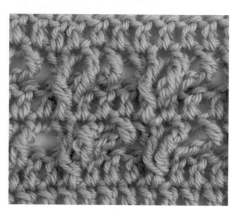

Foundation: Make a multiple of 4 ch.
Row 1: 1 dc in fourth ch from hook, 1 dc in ea ch to end, turn.
Row 2: 3 ch, 1 dc in ea st to end, turn.
Row 3: 3 ch, *skip 3 sts, (1 FPttr, 1 FPdtr, 1 FPtr) around next st on row 2, 1 dc in top of same st, rep from * to last st, 1 dc, turn.
Rep rows 2–3 for required length, ending with row 2.

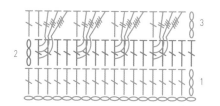

WEDGE—SHORT TO LONG

Foundation: Make a multiple of 4 ch.
Row 1: 1 dc in fourth ch from hook, 1 dc in ea ch to end, turn.
Row 2: 3 ch, 1 dc in ea st to end, turn.
Row 3: 3 ch, *1 dc, (1 FPtr, 1 FPdtr, 1 FPttr) around same st on row 2, skip 3 sts, rep from * to last st, 1 dc, turn.
Rep rows 2–3 for required length, ending with row 2.

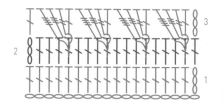

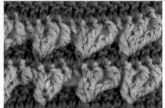

CONTRAST WEDGES

Work as for Wedge-Long to Short but after row 2, change color on every row, to give a textured row in a contrasting yarn.

CONTRAST WEDGES IN BACK LOOP ONLY

Follow the instructions as given for Wedge-Short to Long but read BACK post instead of front post stitches.

ALTERNATING WEDGES

Foundation: Make a multiple of 8 ch + 4.

Row 1: 1 dc in fourth ch from hook, 1 dc in ea ch to end, turn.

Row 2: 3 ch, 1 dc in ea st to end, turn.

Row 3: 3 ch, *skip 3 sts, (1 FPttr, 1 FPdtr, 1 FPtr) around next st on row 2, 1 dc in top of same st, 1 dc, (1 FPtr, 1 FPdtr, 1 FPttr) around next st on row 2, skip 3 sts, rep from * to last st, 1 dc, turn.

Rows 4–5: Rep rows 2–3.

Row 6: Rep row 2.

Row 7: 3 ch, *1 dc, (1 FPtr, 1 FPdtr, 1 FPttr) around same st on row below, skip 6 sts, (1 FPttr, 1 FPdtr, 1 FPtr) around next st on row below, 1 dc in top of same st, rep from * to last st, 1 dc, turn.

Row 8: Rep row 2.

Choose if you are going to rep rows 2–3, or 2–3 and 7–8: rep these rows for required length.

STITCH KEY

chain

$\top$

double crochet

SPECIAL STITCHES

front post treble/
double treble/triple
treble

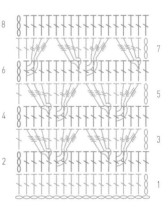

Wings

These motifs have a number of names, "lazy j" and "fairy wings" being the most common. They can be worked starting with either the taller or the shorter stitches, which is useful when you want to make a matching pair. They can also be worked with different numbers of different stitches, increasing or even decreasing the number of stitches along the row.

WINGS (1)

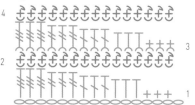

Note: Work the graduated height stitches into the back loop and the crab stitches into the front loop of the previous row.

When starting rows with taller stitches, turning with one chain fewer than is standard gives a neat appearance.

Foundation: Make 16 ch.

Row 1: 1 sc in second ch from hook, 2 sc, 3 hdc, 3 dc, 3 tr, 3 dtr, do not turn.

Row 2: 1 cr st in front loop only of ea st to beginning of row, do not turn.

Row 3: Working in back loop only, 3 sc, 3 hdc, 3 dc, 3 tr, 3 dtr, do not turn.

Rep rows 2–3 once and row 2 once. Fasten off.

WINGS (2)

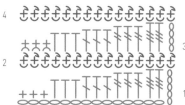

Foundation: Make 19 ch.

Row 1: 1 dtr in sixth ch from hook, 2 dtr, 3 tr, 3 dc, 3 hdc, 3 sc, do not turn.

Row 2: 1 cr st in front loop only of ea st to beginning of row, do not turn.

Row 3: Working in back loop only, 4 ch, 2 dtr, 3 tr, 3 dc, 3 hdc, 3 sc, do not turn.

Rep rows 2–3 once and row 2 once. Fasten off.

CURVED WINGS (1)

Foundation: Make 16 ch.

Row 1: 1 sc in second ch from hook, 4 sc, 2 hdc, 2 hdc in next ch, 2 hdc, 5 dc, do not turn.

Row 2: 1 cr st in front loop only of ea st to beginning of row, do not turn.

Row 3: Working in back loop only, 5 sc, 2 hdc, 2 hdc in next st, 2 hdc, 5 dc, do not turn.

Rep rows 2–3 twice and row 2 once. Fasten off.

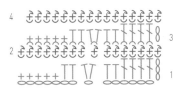

STITCH KEY

For basic stitch symbols, see flap opposite page 95

SPECIAL STITCHES

crab stitch in front loop only

single/half double/double/ crochet in back loop only

treble/double treble crochet in back loop only

2 half doubles in back loop only

2 half doubles together in back loop only (hdc2tog)

CURVED WINGS (2)

Foundation: Make 17 ch.

Row 1: 1 dc in fourth ch from hook, 3 dc, 2 hdc, 2 hdc in next ch, 2 hdc, 5 sc, do not turn.

Row 2: 1 cr st in front loop only of ea st to beginning of row, do not turn.

Row 3: Working in back loop only, 2 ch, 4 dc, 2 hdc, 2 hdc in next st, 2 hdc, 5 sc, do not turn.

Rep rows 2–3 twice and row 2 once. Fasten off.

CURVED WINGS (3)

Foundation: Make 16 ch.

Row 1: 1 sc in second ch from hook, 4 sc, 3 hdc, hdc2tog over next 2 ch, 5 dc, do not turn.

Row 2: 1 cr st in front loop only of ea st to beginning of row, do not turn.

Row 3: Working in back loop only, 5 sc, 2 hdc, hdc2tog over next 2 sts, 5 dc, do not turn.

Row 4: Rep row 2.

Row 5: Working in back loop only, 5 sc, 1 hdc, hdc2tog over next 2 sts, 5 dc, do not turn.

Row 6: Rep row 2.

Row 7: Working in back loop only, 5 sc, hdc2tog over next 2 sts, 5 dc, do not turn.

Row 8: Rep row 2. Fasten off.

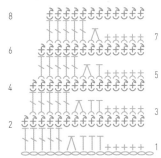

POST STITCHES

Working around the post of stitches instead of into the top two loops (as is the convention) provides many opportunities for the crocheter to create textured surface effects.

Rows

This section shows how working front and back post stitches gives different effects. It's rather like looking at the "right" and "wrong" sides of a double crochet fabric.

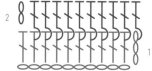

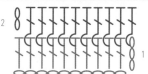

DOUBLE CROCHET FRONT POST STITCHES

Foundation: Make any number of ch.
Row 1: 1 dc in fourth ch from hook, 1 dc in ea ch to end, turn.
Row 2: 2 ch, 1 FPdc around ea st to end, turn.
Rep row 2 for required length.

DOUBLE CROCHET BACK POST STITCHES

Foundation: Make any number of ch.
Row 1: 1 dc in fourth ch from hook, 1 dc in ea ch to end, turn.
Row 2: 2 ch, 1 BPdc around ea st to end, turn.
Rep row 2 for required length.

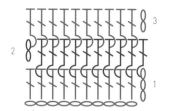

DOUBLE CROCHET ALTERNATING ROWS OF FRONT AND BACK POST STITCHES

Foundation: Make any number of ch.
Row 1: 1 dc in fourth ch from hook, 1 dc in ea ch to end, turn.
Row 2: 2 ch, 1 BPdc around ea st to end, turn.
Row 3: 2 ch, 1 FPdc around ea st to end, turn.
Rep rows 2 and 3 for required length.

TREBLE CROCHET FRONT POST STITCHES

Foundation: Make any number of ch.
Row 1: 1 tr in fifth ch from hook, 1 tr in ea ch to end, turn.
Row 2: 3 ch, 1 FPtr around ea st to end, turn.
Rep row 2 for required length.

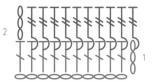

TREBLE CROCHET BACK POST STITCHES

Foundation: Make any number of ch.
Row 1: 1 tr in fifth ch from hook, 1 tr in ea ch to end, turn.
Row 2: 3 ch, 1 BPtr around ea st to end, turn.
Rep row 2 for required length.

TREBLE CROCHET ALTERNATING ROWS OF FRONT AND BACK POST STITCHES

Foundation: Make any number of ch.
Row 1: 1 tr in fifth ch from hook, 1 tr in ea ch to end, turn.
Row 2: 3 ch, 1 BPtr around ea st to end, turn.
Row 3: 3 ch, 1 FPtr around ea st to end, turn.
Rep rows 2 and 3 for required length.

STITCH KEY

chain

double crochet

treble crochet

SPECIAL STITCHES

front post double/treble crochet

back post double/treble crochet

Columns

Having looked at working post stitches in rows on the previous pages, these two pages will concentrate on double crochet post stitches. Have fun exploring this useful mixture of textured effects. Note that if you are going to use the rib fabrics as edgings for garments, you should work out from the item, to make maximum use of the elasticity of the edging.

SINGLE RIB

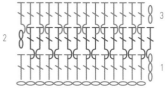

DOUBLE RIB

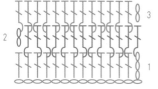

Foundation: Make an odd number of ch.

Row 1: 1 dc in fourth ch from hook, 1 dc in ea ch to end, turn.

Row 2: 2 ch, *1 FPdc around next st on previous row, 1 BPdc around next st on previous row, rep from * to end, turn.

Row 3: 2 ch, *1 BPdc around next st on previous row, 1 FPdc around next st on previous row, rep from * to end, turn.

Rep rows 2 and 3 for the required length.

Foundation: Make a multiple of 4 ch.

Row 1: 1 dc in fourth ch from hook, 1 dc in ea ch to end, turn.

Row 2: 2 ch, 1 BPdc around next st on previous row, *1 FPdc around ea of next 2 sts on previous row, 1 BPdc around ea of next 2 sts on previous row, rep from * to end, turn.

Row 3: 2 ch, 1 FPdc around next st on previous row, *1 BPdc around ea of next 2 sts on previous row, 1 FPdc around ea of next 2 sts on previous row, rep from * to end, turn.

Rep rows 2 and 3 for the required length.

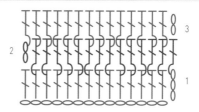

TRIPLE RIB

Foundation: Make a multiple of 6 ch, plus 5.

Row 1: 1 dc in fourth ch from hook, 1 dc in ea ch to end, turn.

Row 2: 2 ch, 1 BPdc around ea of next 2 sts on previous row, *1 FPdc around ea of next 3 sts on previous row, 1 BPdc around ea of next 3 sts on previous row, rep from * to end, turn.

Row 3: 2 ch, 1 FPdc around ea of next 2 sts on previous row, *1 BPdc around ea of next 3 sts on previous row, 1 FPdc around ea of next 3 sts on previous row, rep from * to end, turn.

Rep rows 2 and 3 for the required length.

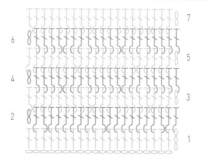

VARIABLE WIDTH COLUMNS

Foundation: Make a multiple of 8 ch, plus 7.

Row 1: 1 dc in fourth ch from hook, 1 dc in ea ch to end, turn.

Row 2: 2 ch, 1 BPdc around next st on previous row, *1 FPdc around next st on previous row, 1 BPdc around ea of next 7 sts on previous row, rep from * to end, omitting 5 BPdc at end of final rep, turn.

Row 3: 2 ch, *1 BPdc around ea of next 3 sts on previous row, 1 FPdc around ea of next 5 sts on previous row, rep from * to end, omitting 4 FPdc at end of final rep, turn.

Row 4: 2 ch, 1 FPdc around ea of next 4 sts on previous row, *1 FPdc around ea of next 3 sts on previous row, 1 FPdc around ea of next 5 sts on previous row, rep from * to end, turn.

Row 5: 2 ch, 1 BPdc around ea of next 5 sts on previous row, *1 FPdc around next st on previous row, 1 BPdc around ea of next 7 sts on previous row, rep from * to end, omitting 1 BPdc at end of final rep, turn.

Row 6: Rep row 4.

Row 7: Rep row 3.

Rep rows 2–7 for required length.

Doubles and Trebles

OFF-SET POST STITCH DOUBLES

Foundation: Make an odd number of ch.
Row 1: 1 sc in second ch from hook, 1 sc in ea ch to end, turn.
Row 2: 1 ch, 1 sc in ea sc to end, turn.
Row 3: 1 ch, 1 sc in next st, *1 FPdc around next st 2 rows below, 1 sc in next st, rep from * to last st, 1 sc turn.
Row 4: Rep row 2.
Row 5: 1 ch, *1 FPdc around next st 2 rows below, 1 sc in next st, rep from * to end, turn.
Rep rows 2–5 for required length.

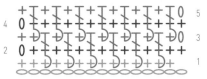

DIAGONALS

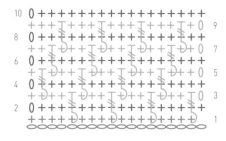

Foundation: Make a multiple of 4 ch, plus 2.
Row 1: 1 sc in second ch from hook, 1 sc in ea sc to end, turn.
Row 2: 1 ch, 1 sc in ea sc to end, turn.
Row 3: 1 ch, *1 FPtr around next st 2 rows below, 3 sc, rep from * to last st, 1 sc, turn.
Row 4: Rep row 2.
Row 5: 1 ch, *3 sc, 1 FPtr in next st 2 rows below, rep from * to last st, 1 sc, turn.

Row 6: Rep row 2.
Row 7: 1 ch, 2 sc, *1 FPtr around next st 2 rows below, 3 sc, rep from * to end, omitting 1 sc at end of final rep.
Row 8: Rep row 2.
Row 9: 1 ch, 1 sc, *1 FPtr around next st 2 rows below, 3 sc, rep from * to end, turn.
Row 10: Rep row 2.
Rep rows 3–10 for required length.

SUBTLE STRIPES

Work as for Off-set Post Stitch Doubles but change color after each odd number row.

HOUNDSTOOTH

Work as for Off-set Post Stitch Doubles but change color after each even number row.

STITCH KEY

o
chain

+
single crochet

CONTRASTING DOUBLES

Work as for Off-set Post Stitch Doubles but change color along the row to pick out the post stitches in a contrast color.

SPECIAL STITCHES

front post
double/treble

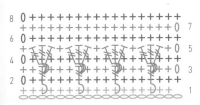

TORCHES

Foundation: Make a multiple of 4 ch, plus 2.
Row 1: 1 sc in second ch from hook, 1 sc in ea ch to end, turn.
Row 2: 1 ch, 1 sc in ea sc to end, turn.
Row 3: 1 ch, 2 sc, *1 FPtr around next st 2 rows below, 3 sc, rep from * to end, omitting 1 sc at end of final rep.
Row 4: Rep row 2.
Row 5: 1 ch, 1 sc, *3 FPtr around next st 2 rows below, skip 3 sts, 1 sc, rep from * to last st, 1 sc, turn.
Rows 6–8: Rep row 2.
Rep rows 3–8 for required length.

3 front post
treble crochets
around same stitch

Basketweave

Regular repeats of front and back post stitches give an almost woven appearance to crocheted fabric. These ideas are further developments of the stitch combinations shown on the previous two pages.

ONE BY ONE BASKETWEAVE

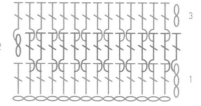

TWO BY TWO BASKETWEAVE

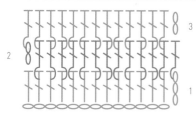

Foundation: Make an odd number of ch.
Row 1: 1 dc in fourth ch from hook, 1 dc in ea ch to end, turn.
Row 2: 2 ch, *1 FPdc around next st on previous row, 1 BPdc around next st on previous row, rep from * to end, turn.
Rep row 2 for the required length.

Foundation: Make a multiple of 4 ch.
Row 1: 1 dc in fourth ch from hook, 1 dc in ea ch to end, turn.
Row 2: 2 ch, 1 BPdc around next st on previous row, *1 FPdc around next 2 sts on previous row, 1 BPdc around next 2 sts on previous row, rep from * to end, turn.
Rep row 2 for the required length.

THREE BY THREE BASKETWEAVE (1)

Foundation: Make a multiple of 6 ch, plus 5.
Row 1: 1 dc in fourth ch from hook, 1 dc in ea ch to end, turn.
Row 2: 2 ch, 1 BPdc around next 2 sts on previous row, *1 FPdc around next 3 sts on previous row, 1 BPdc around next 3 sts on previous row, rep from * to end, turn.
Rep row 2 for the required length.

STITCH KEY

chain

double crochet

THREE BY THREE BASKETWEAVE (2)

Foundation: Make a multiple of 6 ch, plus 5.
Row 1: 1 dc in fourth ch from hook, 1 dc in ea ch to end, turn.
Row 2: 2 ch, 1 BPdc around next 2 sts on previous row, *1 FPdc around next 3 sts on previous row, 1 BPdc around next 3 sts on previous row, rep from * to end, turn.
Row 3: 2 ch, 1 FPdc around next 2 sts on previous row, *1 BPdc around next 3 sts on previous row, 1 FPdc around next 3 sts on previous row, rep from * to end, turn.
Row 4: Rep row 3.
Row 5: Rep row 2.
Rep rows 2–5 for required length.

SPECIAL STITCHES

front post double crochet

back post double crochet

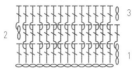

FOUR BY FOUR BASKETWEAVE

Foundation: Make a multiple of 8 ch plus 6.
Row 1: 1 dc in fourth ch from hook, 1 dc in ea ch to end, turn.
Row 2: 2 ch, 1 BPdc around next 3 sts on previous row, *1 FPdc around next 4 sts on previous row, 1 BPdc around next 4 sts on previous row, rep from * to end, turn.

Row 3: 2 ch, 1 FPdc around next 3 sts on previous row, *1 BPdc around next 4 sts on previous row, 1 FPdc around next 4 sts on previous row, rep from * to end, turn.
Rows 4–5: Rep row 2.
Row 6: Rep row 3.
Row 7: Rep row 2.
Rep rows 2–7 for required length.

Puff Stitch

Puff stitches are textured in their own right. Working them as post stitches gives them an additional dimension.

FAUX BULLIONS

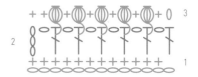

Note: This design uses 5 yo puffs.
Foundation: Make an odd number of ch.
Row 1: 1 sc in second ch from hook, 1 sc in ea ch to end, turn.
Row 2: 4 ch, *skip 1 sc, 1 dc in next st, 1 ch, rep from * to last st, 1 dc, turn.
Row 3: 1 ch, *1 sc in next 1-ch sp, 1 FP puff around next dc, rep from * to last dc, 1 sc in next 2 ch, turn.
Rep rows 2–3 for required length, ending the piece with a row of sc.

SPACED PUFFS

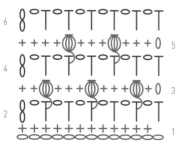

Note: This design uses 5 yo puffs.
Foundation: Make a multiple of 4 ch, plus 1.
Row 1: 1 sc in second ch from hook, 1 sc in ea ch to end, turn.
Row 2: 3 ch, 1 hdc in third sc, *skip next sc, 1ch, 1hdc, rep from * to end, turn.
Row 3: 1 ch, *1 sc in next 1-ch sp, 1 FP puff around next hdc, 1 sc in next 1-ch sp, 1 sc in next hdc, rep from * to end, turn.
Row 4: Rep row 2.
Row 5: 1 ch, *3 sc, 1 FP puff around next hdc, rep from * to end, replacing last FP puff by 1 sc, turn.
Rep rows 2–5 for required length.

SUBTLE PUFFS

Note: This design uses 5 yo puffs.

Foundation: Make an odd number of ch.

Row 1: 1 dc in second ch from hook, *1 sc in next ch, 1 dc in next ch, rep from * to last ch, 1 sc, turn.

Row 2: 2 ch, *1 FP puff around next dc, 1 hdc in next sc, rep from * to end, turn.

Row 3: 1 ch, *1 dc in next puff, 1 sc in next hdc, rep from * to end, turn.

Rep rows 2–3 for required length.

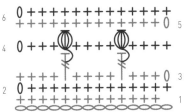

STITCH KEY

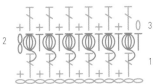

⬭
chain

+
single crochet

T
half double
crochet

†
double crochet

‡
treble crochet

BOLD PUFFS

Note: This design uses 9 yo puffs.

Foundation: Make a multiple of 5 ch, plus 4.

Row 1: 1 sc in second ch from hook, 1 sc in ea ch to end, turn.

Row 2: 1 ch, 1 sc in ea st to end, turn.

Row 3: 1 ch, 3 sc, *1 tr in next st, 4 sc, rep from * to end, turn.

Row 4: 1 ch, 3 sc, *1 FP puff around next tr, 4 sc, rep from * to end, turn.

Rows 5–6: Rep row 2.

Rep rows 3–6 for required length.

SPECIAL STITCHES

front post puff
stitch

HALF DOUBLE CROCHET

Half double crochet has a "yarn over and through three loops on the hook" as its final step, giving an additional horizontal strand to work into.

Simple Textures

Inserting your hook into different parts of the stitch, when working half double crochet makes quite a difference to the surface texture of your work.

Note: When working half double crochet it can often look neater not to count the turning chain as the first stitch because the chains can sometimes result in a bit of a gap or a lack of continuity in the pattern. Try it and see which method you prefer.

FRONT LOOP ONLY

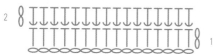

Foundation: Make any number of ch.
Row 1: 1 hdc in third ch from hook, 1 hdc in ea ch to end, turn.
Row 2: 2 ch, 1 hdc in front loop only of same st, 1 hdc in front loop of ea st to end, turn.
Rep row 2 for required length.

BACK LOOP ONLY

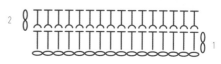

Foundation: Make any number of ch.
Row 1: 1 hdc in third ch from hook, 1 hdc in ea ch to end, turn.
Row 2: 2 ch, 1 hdc in back loop only of same st, 1 hdc in back loop of ea st to end, turn.
Rep row 2 for required length.

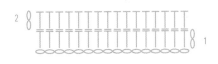

MIDDLE LOOP ONLY
Foundation: Make any number of ch.
Row 1: 1 hdc in third ch from hook, 1 hdc in ea ch to end, turn.

Row 2: 2 ch, 1 hdc in middle loop only of same st, 1 hdc in middle loop of ea st to end, turn.
Rep row 2 for required length.

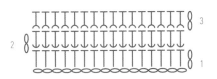

CHAIN LOOK
Foundation: Make any number of ch.
Row 1: 1 hdc in third ch from hook, 1 hdc in ea ch to end, turn.
Row 2: 2 ch, 1 hdc in front loop only of same

st, 1 hdc in front loop of ea st to end, turn.
Row 3: 2 ch, 1 hdc in back loop only of same st, 1 hdc in back loop of ea st to end, turn.
Rep rows 2–3 for required length.

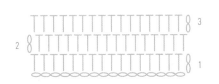

WORKING BETWEEN THE STITCHES
Note: In this design, standard hdc is worked between the stitches, instead of into the top of the stitch in the normal way.
Foundation: Make any number of ch—work loosely, as this stitch expands sideways.

Row 1: 1 hdc in third ch from hook, 1 hdc in ea ch to end, turn.
Row 2: 2 ch, 1 hdc in the gap before ea st to end, 1 hdc in last hdc, turn.
Rep row 2 for required length.

STITCH KEY

⊘
chain

⊤
half double crochet

SPECIAL STITCHES

⊥
half double crochet in front loop only

I
half double crochet in middle loop only

⊥
half double crochet in back loop only

Three-fold Fabrics

The unique three-loop top of the half double crochet can be exploited in a number of ways.

JUST PEACHY

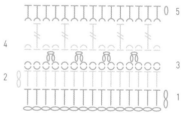

Foundation: Make a multiple of 3 ch + 2.
Row 1: 1 hdc in third ch from hook, 1 hdc in ea ch to end, turn.
Row 2: 2 ch, 1 hdc in ea hdc to end, turn.
Row 3: (no turning ch) Working in front loop only, 3 sl st, *3 ch, do not skip any sts, 3 sl st, rep from * to end, turn.
Row 4: (no turning ch) Working in middle loop only of row 2, *1 sl st, 1 tr, 1 sl st, rep from * to end, turn.
Row 5: 1 ch, working in back loop only of row 2, 1 hdc in ea hdc to end, turn.
Rep rows 2–5 for required length.

CORNFIELD

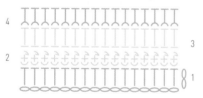

Note: The yarns not in use should be stranded loosely up the sides of the rows.
Foundation: Using color A, make any number of ch.
Row 1: 1 hdc in third ch from hook, 1 hdc in ea ch to end, change to color B in last st, do not turn, do not break off yarn.
Row 2: 1 cr st in front loop only of ea st to end, change to color C in last st, do not turn, do not break off yarn.
Row 3: 1 hdc in middle loop only of ea st in row 1, change to color A in last st, do not turn, do not break off yarn.
Row 4: 1 hdc in ea ch to end, change to color B in last st, do not turn, do not break off yarn.
Rep rows 2–4 for required length.

RUSTY

Foundation: Make an even number of ch.

Row 1: 1 hdc in third ch from hook, 1 hdc in ea ch to end, turn.

Row 2: Working in back loop only, *1 sl st, 3ch, do not skip any sts, 1 sl st, rep from * to end, turn.

Row 3: Working in middle loop only of row 1, 1 sl st, *1 sl st, 3ch, do not skip any sts, 1 sl st, rep from * to last st, 1 sl st, turn.

Row 4: Working in back loop only of row 1, 1 hdc in ea st to end, turn.

Row 5: Working in front loop only, *1 sl st, 3ch, do not skip any sts, 1 sl st, rep from * to end, turn.

Rows 6–7: Rep rows 3–4.

Rep rows 2–7 for required length.

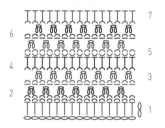

STITCH KEY

slip stitch

chain

half double crochet

SPECIAL STITCHES

crab stitch

slip stitch/single crochet /crab stitch in front loop only

slip stitch/half double/treble crochet in middle loop only

slip stitch/half double crochet in back loop only

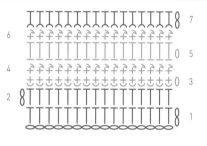

THREE-FOLD ROWS

This design uses three colors (A, B, and C). Change color where directed and strand the spare yarns loosely up the side of the work.

Note: This design works best if the turning chains do not replace the first stitch on the row.

Foundation: Using color A, make any number of ch.

Row 1: 1 hdc in third ch from hook, 1 hdc in ea ch to end, turn.

Row 2: 2 ch, 1 hdc in ea st to end, change to color B at the end of the row, turn.

Row 3: 1 ch, 1 sc in front loop of ea st to end, do not turn.

Row 4: 1 cr st in ea st to end, change to color C at the end of the row, do not turn.

Row 5: 1 ch, 1 hdc in middle loop only of ea st in row 2 to end, do not turn.

Row 6: Rep row 4, change to color A at end of row.

Row 7: 2 ch, 1 hdc, in back loop only of ea st in row 2 to end.

Rep rows 2–7 for required length.

In the Round

Half double crochet can be used for circular patterns and motifs such as these.

SPIRAL

Note: In this design, the rounds are not closed with a slip stitch. It may be helpful to mark the beginning of each round with a contrast thread.
Foundation: Make a slip knot that pulls up from the tail end (see page 10), 3 ch.
Round 1: 8 hdc in third ch from hook, do not join the round, do not turn.
Round 2: Working in the back loop only, 2 hdc in ea st to end, do not join the round, do not turn.
Round 3: Working in the back loop only, (1 hdc, 2 hdc in next st) 8 times, do not join the round, do not turn.
Round 4: Working in the back loop only, (2 hdc, 2 hdc in next st) 8 times, do not join the round, do not turn.
Round 5: Working in the back loop only, (3 hdc, 2 hdc in next st) 7 times, 1 sc, 1 sl st. Fasten off. Gently pull the starting yarn to close the hole at the center, sew in end. Fasten off.

LOOPY FLOWER

Foundation: Using color A, make a slip knot that pulls up from the tail end (see page 10), 3 ch.
Round 1: 8 hdc in third ch from hook, 1 sl st in first hdc.
Round 2: Working in front loop only, 1 ch, (1 sc, 3 ch, 1 sc) in ea hdc to end, 1 sl st in first sc. Fasten off.
Round 3: Join in color B, working in middle loop only of round 1, (1 sc, 7 ch, 1 sc) in ea st to end, 1 sl st in first sc. Fasten off.
Round 4: Join in color C, working in back loop only of round 1, (1 sc, 11 ch, 1 sc) in ea st to end, 1 sl st in first sc. Fasten off.

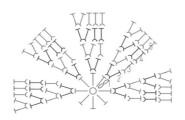

CRAZY FLOWER

Foundation: Make a slip knot that pulls up from the tail end, 3 ch.

Round 1: 36 hdc in third ch from hook, 1 sl st in first hdc.

Round 2: 1 ch, *1 sl st, 5 hdc in next st, rep from * to end, sl st in first sl st. Fasten off.

After the center loop has been tightened and secured, arrange the petals in a way that pleases you.

STITCH KEY

For basic stitch symbols, see flap opposite page 95

SPECIAL STITCHES

single/half double in front loop only

single/double in middle loop only

single/half double in back loop only

double/treble in back loop only

5 half double crochets in same stitch

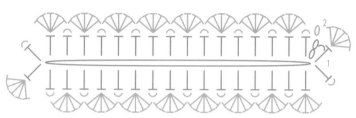

ROSETTE

Note: This pattern makes a very full rosette, and it only just lies flat. For neatness, the rounds are joined when the yarn ends are sewn in.

Foundation: Using color A, make a slip knot that pulls up from the tail end, 3 ch.

Round 1: 8 hdc in third ch from hook, 1 sl st in first hdc.

Round 2: Working in front loop only, 2 ch, (1 hdc, 3 ch, sl st in first of these ch) in ea st to end. Fasten off.

Round 3: Working in middle loop only of round 1, join in color B, 3 ch, (1 dc, 4 ch,

sl st in first of these ch) twice in ea st to end. Fasten off.

Round 4: Working in back loop only of round 1, join in color C, 4 ch, (1 tr, 5 ch, sl st in first of these ch) three times in ea st to end. Fasten off.

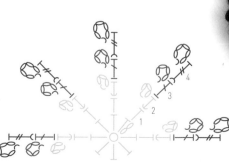

LONG TREBLES

Fabrics made of only long trebles can be somewhat unstable, but worked as post stitches with more standard length stitches, they provide a range of possibilities to create textures.

Boxes

Long trebles worked as post stitches can be used to create textured box effects.

Note: Colors not in use should be stranded loosely up the side of the work

BASIC BOXES

Foundation: Using color A, make a multiple of 8 ch + 2.
Row 1: 1 dc in fourth ch from hook, 1 dc in ea st to end, turn.
Row 2: 3 ch, 1 dc in ea st to end, change color at end of row, but do not fasten off color A, turn.
Rows 3–4: Rep row 2 (in color B), change to color A at end of row 4, do not fasten off color B, turn.
Row 5: 3 ch, 2 dc, *(1 FPquadtr around next st on row 2) twice, 6 dc, rep from * to end, omitting 3 dc at end of last rep, turn.
Rep rows 2–5 for required length, ending with row 5.

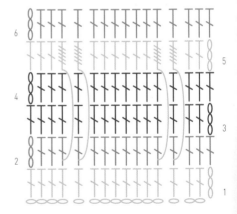

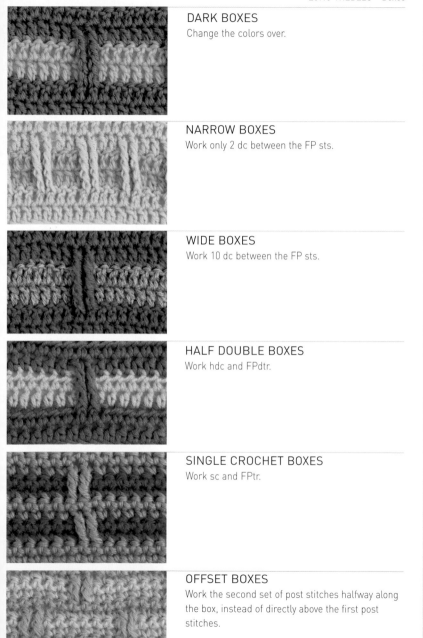

DARK BOXES
Change the colors over.

NARROW BOXES
Work only 2 dc between the FP sts.

WIDE BOXES
Work 10 dc between the FP sts.

HALF DOUBLE BOXES
Work hdc and FPdtr.

SINGLE CROCHET BOXES
Work sc and FPtr.

OFFSET BOXES
Work the second set of post stitches halfway along the box, instead of directly above the first post stitches.

STITCH KEY

O

chain

T

double crochet

SPECIAL STITCHES

front post quadruple treble

Color Blending

A wide range of color blending effects is possible—use yarns of similar weights, use up your yarn oddments, and have fun with this technique. Changing color on every row does leave a lot of ends to manage, but the fabric produced is worth the effort.

BASIC BLENDING

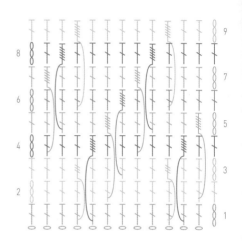

Note: Change color at the end of every row.
Foundation: Make a multiple of 6 ch + 3.
Row 1: 1 dc in fourth ch from hook, 1 dc in ea ch to end, turn.
Row 2: 3 ch, 1 dc in ea st to end, turn.
Row 3: 3 ch, 2 dc, *1 FPdtr around next st in row 1, 5 dc, rep from * to end, omitting 2 dc at end of last rep, turn.
Row 4: 3 ch, 3 dc, *1 BPttr around next st on row 1, 5 dc, rep from * to end, omitting 3 dc at end of last rep, turn.
Row 5: 3 ch, *1 FPquadtr around next st on row 2, 5 dc, rep from * to end, turn.
Row 6: 3 ch, *5 dc, 1 BPquadtr around next st on row 3, rep from * to end omitting final BP st, turn.

Row 7: 3 ch, 4 dc, *1 FPquadtr around next st on row 4, 5 dc, rep from * to end omitting 4 dc at end of last rep, turn.
Row 8: 3 ch, 1 dc, *1 BPquadtr around next st on row 5, 5 dc, rep from * to end, omitting 1 dc at end of last rep, turn.
Row 9: 3 ch, 2 dc, *1 FPquadtr around next st on row 6, 5 dc, rep from * to end, omitting 2 dc at end of last rep, turn.
Rep rows 4–9 for required length.

ALLOVER COLOR BLENDING

Note: Change color at the end of every row.
Foundation: Make a multiple of 6 ch + 3.
Row 1: 1 dc in fourth ch from hook, 1 dc in ea ch to end, turn.
Row 2: 3 ch, 1 dc in ea st to end, turn.
Row 3: 3 ch, 2 dc, *1 FPdtr around next st in row 1, 2 dc, rep from * to last st, 1 dc, turn.
Row 4: 3 ch, *1 BPttr around next st on row 1, 2 dc, rep from * to end, turn.
Row 5: 3 ch, *1 FPquadtr around next st on row 2, 2 dc, rep from * to end, turn.
Row 6: 3 ch, *2 dc, 1 BPquadtr around next st on row 3, rep from * to last st, 1 dc, turn.
Row 7: 3 ch, 1 dc, *1 FPquadtr around next st on row 4, 2 dc, rep from * to end omitting 1 dc at end of last rep, turn.
Row 8: 3 ch, 1 dc, *1 BPquadtr around next st on row 5, 2 dc, rep from * to end, omitting 1 dc at end of last rep, turn.
Row 9: 3 ch, 2 dc, *1 FPquadtr around next st on row 6, 2 dc, rep from * to last st, 1 dc, turn.
Rep rows 4–9 for required length.

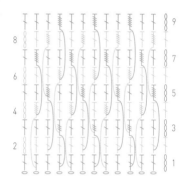

STITCH KEY

○
chain

T
half double crochet

╤
double crochet

╪
treble crochet

SPECIAL STITCHES

front post double treble/quadruple treble/quintuple treble

back post double treble/ triple treble

back post quadruple treble

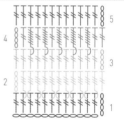

COLOR BLENDING STRIPES

Foundation: Using color A, make an even number of ch.
Row 1: 1 tr in fifth ch from hook, 1 tr in ea ch to end, change to color B color at end of row, but do not fasten off, turn.
Row 2: 4 ch, *1 FPdtr around next st on row 1, 1 BPdtr around next st on row 1, rep from * to last 2 sts, 1 FPdtr around next st on row 1, 1 tr, turn.
Row 3: 4 ch, 1 tr in ea st to end, change to color A at end of row, but do not fasten off, turn.
Row 4: 4 ch, *1 tr, 1 FPquintr around next st on row 3, rep from * to last 2 sts, 2 tr, turn.
Row 5: 4 ch, 1 tr in ea st to end, change to color B at end of row, but do not fasten off, turn.
Rep rows 2–5 for required length.

Diagonals

Long trebles can be very useful and interesting when they are offset from the vertical. Having long unsupported stitches means that these fabrics are not ideal for garments in everyday use, but they add an extra dimension to hangings and other artworks.

ZIGZAGS (1)

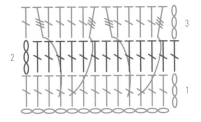

ZIGZAGS (2)

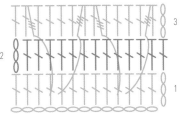

Foundation: Make a multiple of 6 ch + 4.
Row 1: 1 dc in fourth ch from hook, 1 dc in ea st to end, turn.
Row 2: 3 ch, 1 dc in ea st to end, turn.
Row 3: 3 ch, * 1 FPdtr around third dc along on row 1, skip 1 st, 4 dc, 1 FPdtr around st on row 1 after the last FPdtr, skip 1 st, rep from * to last st, 1 dc, turn.
Rep rows 2–3 for required length, ending with row 2.

Note: Softly spun yarns benefit from having extra support at the point where the post stitches are worked. This is achieved by working the post stitch to the last yo, then working a background st in the st that would otherwise be skipped to the same point, before working the two stitches off as a single stitch in the manner of a cluster.
Work as for Zigzags (1), but use the following instructions for row 3.
Row 3: 3 ch, *1 dc and 1 FPdtr around fourth st along on row 1, skip 1 st, 4 dc, (work a cluster of 1 dc and 1 FPdtr around st on row 1 after the last FPdtr), rep from * to last st, 1 dc, turn.

"V" COLUMNS

Work as for Zigzags (2) but work a number of dc between each v-shaped pair of post stitches.

chain

CLOSE COLUMNS

Follow the pattern for either Zigzags (1) or Zigzags (2) but omit plain dc rows after row 1 and work alternate rows with BP sts.

double crochet

MOCK CABLES

Follow the pattern for either Zigzags (1) or Zigzags (2) but work single columns of post stitches, with a number of dc between them—remember that the stitches can slant in either direction.

SPECIAL STITCHES

front post double treble/ quadruple treble

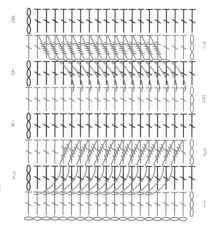

MOCK ROPES

In a plain dc fabric, work one of the following rows to produce horizontal rows of post stitches. Long post stitches allow you to work further forward or back, which the previous pattern does not.

Sloping up to the right: 3 ch, (1 dc and work a cluster of 1 FPquadtr around fifth dc along 2 rows below) to last 5 sts, 5 dc, turn.

Sloping up to the left: 3 ch, 4 dc, (work a cluster of 1 FPquadtr around second st along 2 rows below and 1 dc) to last st, 1 dc, turn.

Trees

These designs take a single idea and play with it, providing a variety of results that would produce a lovely "Fair Isle" style item, without having to adjust for different stitch gauges.

TREES (1)

Note: Change color along the row to make the post stitches in a contrasting color.
Foundation: Make a multiple of 9 ch + 1.
Row 1: 1 sc in second ch from hook, 1 sc in ea ch to end, turn.
Row 2: 1 ch, 1 sc in ea st to end, turn.
Row 3: 1 ch, *3 sc, 1 FPdc around next st on row 2 twice, 4 sc, rep from * to end, turn.
Row 4: Rep row 2.
Row 5: 1 ch, *3 sc, 1 FPtr around sc before FPdc on row 3, 1 FPtr around sc after second FPdc on row 3, 4 sc, rep from * to end, turn.

Row 6: Rep row 2.
Row 7: 1 ch, *3 sc, 1 FPdtr around sc before FPdtr on row 4, 1 FPdtr around sc after FPdc on row 4, 4 sc, rep from * to end, turn.
Row 8: Rep row 2.
Row 9: 1 ch, *3 sc, 1 FPttr around sc before FPdtr on row 5, 1 FPttr around sc after FPdtr on row 5, 4 sc, rep from * to end, turn.
Rows 10–11: Rep row 2.
Rep rows 2–11 for required length.

TREES (2)

Work four rows of sc, then Trees (1) rows as follows: 1, 2, 9, 4, 7, 6, 5. 8, 3, 10, 11.

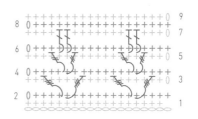

STITCH KEY

TREES (3)

Note: Change color along the row to make the post stitches in a contrasting color.
Foundation: Make a multiple of 9 ch + 1.
Row 1: 1 sc in second ch from hook, 1 sc in ea ch to end, turn.
Row 2: 1 ch, 1 sc in ea st to end, turn.
Row 3: 1 ch, *(work a cluster of 1 sc and 1 FPdtr around fourth sc on row 2), 6 sc, (work a cluster of 1 FPdtr around st next to last FPdtr on row 2), rep from * to last st, 1 sc, turn.
Row 4: Rep row 2.
Row 5: 1 ch, *1 sc, (work a cluster of 1 sc and 1 FPtr around third sc on row 4), 4 sc, (work a cluster of 1 FPtr around st next to

last FPtr on row 4), 2 sc, rep from * to end, turn.
Row 6: Rep row 2.
Row 7: 1 ch, *2 sc, (work a cluster of 1 sc and 1 FPtr around second sc on row 6), 2 sc, (work a cluster of 1 FPtr around st next to last FPtr on row 4), 3 sc, rep from * to end, turn.
Row 8: Rep row 2.
Row 9: 1 ch, *3 sc, 1 FPdc around next sc on row 8, twice, 4 sc, rep from * to end, turn.
Rows 10–11: Rep row 2.
Rep rows 2–11 for required length.

chain

+
single crochet

SPECIAL STITCHES

front post double/ treble

front post double treble/triple treble

TREES (4)

For this variation you could use the patterns for either Trees (1) or Trees (3) as a basis. Work rows in this order: 1, 2, 9, 4, 7, 6, 5, 8, 3, 10, 11.
Note: For short trees, work four extra rows of plain sc before starting the variation.

TREES (5)

For this variation you could use the patterns for either Trees (1) or Trees (3) as a basis. Work as per chart of your choice, but use the longest FP st listed in the instructions, wherever an FP st is stated.

The texture of many of the designs in this book is worked over a single row; extending this to two or more rows opens up even more possibilities—here are a few.

Two-row Textures

A simple two-row bobble idea is explored in these designs. All but the very big bobbles can be used in almost any situation—the largest bobbles may be a little more heavyweight and hence could be vulnerable to damage in wear.

CHESTNUTS

Foundation: Make a multiple of 6 ch, plus 3.
Row 1: 1 dc in fourth ch from hook, 1 dc in ea ch to end turn.
Row 2: 3 ch, 1 dc in ea st to end, turn.
Row 3: 3 ch, 2 dc, *5 dc in next st, 5 dc, rep from * to end, omitting 2 dc at end of final rep, turn.
Row 4: 3 ch, 2 dc, *dc5tog, 5 dc, rep from * to end, omitting 2 dc at end of final rep, turn.
Row 5: Rep row 2.
Rep rows 2–5 for required length.

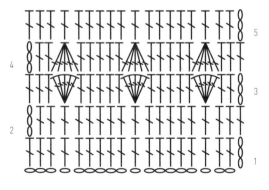

GARDEN FLOWERS

Change color along rows 3 and 4, to work "leaves" in green and "flowers" in a suitable color.

STRAWBERRIES IN A ROW

Change color along rows 3 and 4 to make the berries red and the hulls green.

chain

double crochet

ALLOVER FLOWERS

Offset alternate rows of flowers, to form them in the middle stitch between the previous row of flowers.

SPECIAL STITCHES

5 double crochets in same stitch (fan)

FLOURISHING FLOWERS

Maintain the 5-dc fan, but replace the dc5tog with tr5tog.

5 double crochets together (dc5tog)

BIG BOBBLES

Work both top and bottom of bobbles using tr.

LUSCIOUS FRUITS

This variation places the bobbles to resemble a display of fruit, replace the 5-dc fan with a 5-tr fan.

Delicate Effects

This section explores the possibilities offered by changing the height of stitches along a row, the number of stitches along a row, or both. The effects are not particularly dramatic, nor are the hollow "eruptions" from the surface as robust as some, but they may be useful nonetheless.

SUBTLE STITCH TEXTURE

Foundation: Make a multiple of 11 ch, plus 8.
Row 1: 1 sc in second ch from hook, 1 sc in ea ch to end, turn.
Row 2: 1 ch, 1 sc in ea st to end, turn.
Row 3: 1 ch, 2 sc, *1 hdc, 3 dc, 1 hdc, 3 sc, rep from * to end, turn.
Rows 4–5: Rep row 3.
Rows 6–8: Rep row 2.
Row 9: 1 ch, 6 sc, *1 hdc, 3 dc, 1 hdc, 3 sc, rep from * to last 4 sts, 4 sc, turn.
Rows 10–11: Rep row 9.
Rows 12–14: Rep row 2.
Rep rows 3–14 for required length.

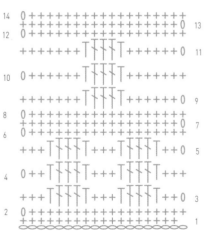

ENHANCED STITCH TEXTURE

Foundation: Make a multiple of 6 ch, plus 3.
Row 1: 1 dc in fourth ch from hook, 1 dc in ea ch to end, turn.
Row 2: 3 ch, 1 dc in ea st to end, turn.
Row 3: 3 ch, 2 dc, *5 dc in next st, 5 dc, rep from * to end, omitting 2 dc at end of final rep, turn.
Row 4: Rep row 2.
Row 5: 3 ch, 2 dc, *dc5tog, 5 dc, rep from * to end, omitting 2 dc at end of final rep, turn.
Rows 6–7: Rep row 2.
Rep rows 2–7 for required length.

TALL AND THIN STITCH TEXTURE

Note: This design was made by changing color along the row to make only the tr in the contrast yarn.
Foundation: Make a multiple of 3 ch.
Row 1: 1 dc in fourth ch from hook, 1 dc in ea ch to end, turn.
Row 2: 3 ch, 1 dc in ea st to end, turn.
Row 3: 3 ch, 2 dc, *3 tr in next st, 2 dc, rep from * to last st, 1 dc, turn.
Row 4: 3 ch, 2 dc, *3 tr, 2 dc, rep from * to last st, 1 dc, turn.
Row 5: 3 ch, 2 dc, *tr3tog, 2 dc, rep from * to last st, 1 dc, turn.
Rows 6–7: Rep row 2.
Rep rows 2–7 for required length.

STITCH KEY

For basic stitch symbols, see flap opposite page 95

SPECIAL STITCHES

5 double crochets in same stitch

5 double crochets together (dc5tog)

3 treble crochets in same stitch

3 treble crochets together (tr3tog)

Working Extra Fabric

This section explores the possibilities offered by working a length of chain on one row and including the extra fabric in at least two subsequent rows. When using the charts, you will need to work from both the main chart and the supplementary chart for each design.

SOLID BOBBLES

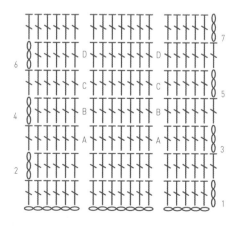

Note: The bobbles are made more solid by slip stitching each round on the bobble back into the base fabric.

Foundation: Make 21 ch.

Row 1: 1 dc in fourth ch from hook, 1 dc in ea ch to end, turn.

Row 2: 3 ch, 1 dc in ea st to end, turn.

Row 3: 3 ch, 5 dc, 9 ch, 1 sl st in last dc worked, 7 dc, 9 ch, 1 sl st in last dc worked, 6 dc, turn.

Row 4: 3 ch, 5 dc, *9 dc in ch, 1 sl st in last dc worked, 7 dc, rep from * omitting 1 dc at end of last rep, turn.

Row 5: 3 ch, 5 dc, *dc3tog 3 times, 1 sl st in last dc worked, 7 dc, rep from * omitting 1 dc at end of last rep, turn.

Row 6: 3 ch, 5 dc, *sl st in center dc3tog on ch, 7 dc, rep from * omitting 1 dc at end of last rep, turn.

Row 7: Rep row 2. Fasten off.

Read each line of the supplementary chart (below) from right to left

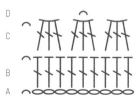

BELLS

Foundation: Make 19 ch.

Row 1: 1 sc in second ch from hook, 1 sc in ea ch to end, turn.

Row 2: 1 ch, 1 sc in ea st to end, turn.

Rows 3–5: Rep row 2.

Row 6: 1 ch, 5 sc, 12 ch, sl st in last st worked, 7 sc, 12 ch, sl st in last sc worked, 6 sc, turn.

Row 7: 1 ch, 5 sc, (1 sc, hdc2tog, dc3tog six times, hdc2tog, 1 sc) in ch, sl st in last sc, 7 sc worked, (1 sc, hdc2tog, dc3tog six times, hdc2tog, 1 sc) in ch, sl st in last sc worked, 6 sc, turn.

Row 8: 1 ch, 5 sc, (1 sc, 1 hdc, 6 dc 1 hdc, 1 sc) in sts on ch, sl st in last sc worked on main fabric, 7 sc, (1 sc, 1 hdc, 6 dc 1 hdc, 1 sc) in sts on ch, sl st in last sc worked on main fabric, 6 sc, turn.

Row 9: Rep row 8.

Row 10: 1 ch, 5 sc, (sc2tog, dc2tog 3 times, sc2tog) in sts on ch, 7 sc, (sc2tog, dc2tog 3 times, sc2tog) in sts on ch, 6 sc, turn.

Rows 11–13: Rep row 2. Fasten off.

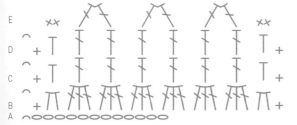

Read each line of the supplementary chart (left) from right to left

STITCH KEY

⌒
slip stitch

◯
chain

+
single crochet

T
half double crochet

T
double crochet

SPECIAL STITCHES

✗✗
2 single crochets in same stitch

ⵏ ⵏ
2/3 double crochet together

These pages introduce you to just a few of the ways you can combine some of the stitches you have seen in other parts of this book.

Diamonds and Blooms

Once you have mastered the techniques in the rest of the book, you can experiment with all sorts of combinations of the techniques, or even make your own crochet interpretation of a favorite knitted Aran item. The uses for Aran combination stitch fabrics are without limit.

DIAMOND BLOOM

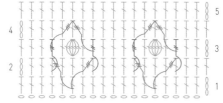

Foundation: Multiple of 8 plus 5 chains.

Row 1: 1 dc in fourth ch from hook, 1 dc in each ch to end, turn.

Row 2: 3 ch, 1 dc in next 2 sts, *work cluster as follows, (1 dc and 1 BPdtr around third stitch along on row below), 3 dc, work cluster as follows, (1 BPdtr around the same st as the BPdtr worked earlier in the row and 1 dc in next stitch), 3 dc, rep from * to end, turn.

Row 3: 3ch, 1 dc in next 2 sts, *work cluster as follows, (1 FPtr around the BPdtr in the row below and 1 dc in next stitch), 1 dc, work 1 5-dc bobble in next st, 1 dc, work cluster as follows, (1 dc in next stitch and 1 FPtr around BPdtr in the row below), 3 dc, rep from * to end, turn.

Row 4: 3 ch, *1 dc in next 4 sts, work cluster as follows (1 BPdtr around FPtr in the row below, 1 dc in top of bobble, 1 BPdtr around FPtr in the row below), 3 dc, rep from * to last 2 sts, 2 dc, turn.

Row 5: 3 ch, 1 dc in each st to end, 3 ch, turn. Rep rows 2–5 for required length, ending with row 4. Omit tch at end of final row.

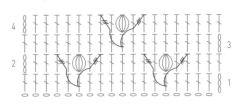

chain

double crochet

ARAN BLOOM

Foundation: Multiple of 16 plus 5 chains.
Row 1: 1 dc in third ch from hook, 1 dc in each ch to end, turn.
Row 2: 3 ch, 1 dc in next 2 sts, *work cluster as follows, (1 dc and 1 BPdtr around third stitch along on row below), 1 dc, work 1 5-loop puff stitch in next st, 1 dc, work cluster as follows, (1 BPdtr around the same st as the BPdtr worked earlier in the row and 1 dc in next stitch), 3 dc, rep from * to end, turn.

Row 3: 3 ch, 1 dc in each st to end, 3 ch, turn.
Row 4: 3 ch, 1 dc in next 6 sts, *work cluster as follows, (1 dc and 1 BPdtr around third stitch along on row below), 1 dc, work 1 5-loop puff stitch in next st, 1 dc, work cluster as follows, (1 BPdtr around the same st as the BPdtr worked earlier in the row and 1 dc), 5 dc, rep from * to last 2 sts, 2 dc, turn. Rep rows 1–4 for required length. Omit tch at end of final row.

SPECIAL STITCHES

front post treble crochet

back post double treble crochet

bobble

puff stitch

IN FULL BLOOM

Work as for Aran Bloom but replace the 5-loop puff with a 9-loop puff and replace the post stitch clusters with just a post stitch and skip the stitch that you've used for the post stitch.

BOBBLE BLOOM

Work as for Aran Bloom, but replace the puff with a 7-dc bobble. Also when working the post stitch clusters, swap the order of the stitches, i.e. where you made the double crochet first, work the post stitch as the first part of the cluster (and vice versa).

FAN BLOOM

Work as for Aran Bloom but replace the puff stitch with a 5-dc fan (i.e. work 5 dc in the stitch instead of the puff). When working the next row, put 1 dc in the last dc of the fan.

Cables

One of the most characteristic stitch combinations in Aran knitting is the cable. When working cables in crochet, you can make the cable slope to the left or the right, depending on whether you work in front or behind the skipped stitches.

CROSSED STITCH CABLE SAMPLER

Note: See page 13 for working edc.
Foundation: Make 26 ch.
Row 1: 1 dc in fourth ch from hook, 1 dc in ea of next 2 ch, skip next ch, 1 edc in next ch, 1 edc in skipped ch, 3 dc, skip 2 ch, 1 tr in ea of next 2 ch, 1 tr in ea of skipped ch, 3 dc, skip 3 ch, 1 etr in ea of next 3 ch, 1 etr in ea of skipped ch, 3 dc, turn.
Row 2: 3 ch, 2 dc, skip 3 sts, 1 etr in ea of next 3 sts, 1 etr in ea of skipped sts, 3 dc, skip 2 sts, 1 tr in ea of next 2 sts, 1 tr in ea of skipped sts, 3 dc, skip 1 st, 1 edc in next st, 1 edc in skipped st, 3 dc, turn.
Row 3: 3 ch, 1 dc in ea of next 2 sts, skip next st, 1 edc in next st, 1 edc in skipped st, 3 dc, skip 2 sts, 1 tr in ea of next 2 sts, 1 tr in ea of skipped sts, 3 dc, skip 3 sts, 1 edc in ea of next 3 sts, 1 edc in ea of skipped sts, 3 dc, turn.
Rep rows 2 and 3 for required length.

POST STITCH CABLE

Foundation: Make a multiple of 7 ch plus 5.
Row 1: 1 dc in fourth ch from hook, 1 dc in ea ch to end, turn.
Row 2: 3 ch, 1 dc in ea st to end, turn.
Row 3: 3 ch, 2 dc, *skip 2 sts, 1 FPdtr in ea of next 2 sts in second row down, 1 FPdtr in ea of skipped sts in second row down, 3 dc, rep from * to end, turn.
Rep rows 2 and 3 for required length.

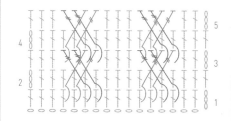

HALFWAY HOUSE CABLE

Work as for Post Stitch Cable, but replace the stitches at the back of the cable with treble crochet, not post stitches.

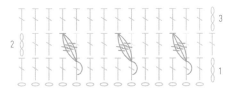

BOBBLE CABLE

Foundation: Make a multiple of 4 ch + 1.
Row 1: 1 dc in fourth ch from hook, 1 dc in ea ch to end, turn.
Row 2: 3 ch, *2 dc, skip 1 st, FPtr3tog around next st on row below, 1 dc in top of same st, rep from * to last 2 sts, 2 dc, turn.
Row 3: 3 ch, 1 dc in ea st to end, turn.
Rep rows 2 and 3 for required length.

COLORED BOBBLE CABLE

Work as for Bobble Cable but change color along the row, working the bobble, and then the dc in the top of the same stitch in a contrasting color.

STITCH KEY

chain

double crochet

SPECIAL STITCHES

extended double crochet

extended treble crochet

front post treble/ double treble

front post bobble (FPtr3tog)

TAKING IT FURTHER

There are numerous ways of adding textural interest to your crochet. This section gives you a whistle-stop tour of some of the further possibilities.

Curlicues

A double crochet background has been used here for ease and speed of working, but you may choose any plain crochet stitch for the main fabric. Vertical and horizontal spacing may also be adjusted, giving a great variety of textured effects.

CURLICUE SWIRLS

Foundation: Make a multiple of 5 ch, plus 2.
Row 1: 1 dc in fourth ch from hook, 1 dc in ea ch to end, turn.
Row 2: 3 ch, 1 dc in ea st to end, turn.
Row 3: 3 ch, 4 dc, *10 ch, 2 dc in fourth ch from hook, 3 dc in ea of next 6 ch, sl st in top of last dc worked in main fabric, 5 dc, rep from * to end, turn.
Row 4: Rep row 2.
Row 5: 3 ch, 2 dc, *10 ch, 2 dc in fourth ch from hook, 3 dc in ea of next 6 ch, sl st in top of last dc worked in main fabric, 5 dc, rep from * to end, omitting last 3 dc of final rep, turn.
Rep rows 2–5 for required length, end with a dc row.

▲ Wherever this symbol occurs work the following:

DAINTY SWIRLS

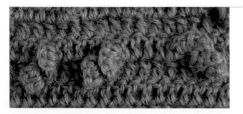

Using the same spacing, for each swirl work 6 ch, 2 sc in second ch from hook, 3 sc in rem swirl ch.

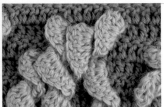

CONTRAST SWIRLS
Change color for the curlicues only. This sample also uses 7, 10, and 13 ch for the swirls, worked with 3 dc in ea ch.

GRADUATED SWIRLS
This sample shows what happens when you work 3 sc, 3 hdc, 3 dc, 3 tr, 3 dtr into the curlicue of 6 ch.

ANCHORED SWIRLS
In the first row of swirls, the ends of the completed curlicues are stitched down after the work has been completed. The top row of swirls is attached to the base in various positions with sl st as the work progresses.

FURRY SWIRLS
Work sc curlicues with 6 ch in alternate stitches on each row.

CHUNKY SWIRLS
This sample uses 7 sc or 7 dc in curlicue chains of varying lengths. Unless you artificially increase the size of each chain, this is the maximum amount of stitches you can work in each chain.

Popcorns

A popcorn is a cluster of three, four, or five double crochet stitches, that provide a range of highly textured effects. The designs on these pages will help you to start exploring these possibilities.

ALLOVER POPCORNS
Note: This design uses 3-dc popcorns.
Foundation: Make an odd number of ch.
Row 1: pc in fifth ch from hook, *skip 1 ch, pc in next ch, rep from * to end, turn.
Row 2: 3 ch, pc in ea pc to end, turn.
Rep row 2 for required length.

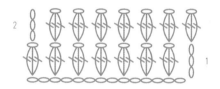

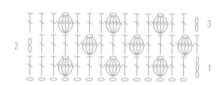

WIDE-SPACED POPCORNS
Note: This design uses 5-dc popcorns.
Foundation: Make a multiple of 4 ch, plus 1.
Row 1: 1 dc in fourth ch from hook, 1 dc in next ch, *pc in next ch, 1 dc in ea of next 3 ch, rep from * to end, turn.

Row 2: 3 ch, *1 pc in next dc, 1 dc in ea of next 3 sts, rep from * to end, omitting 2 dc at end of final rep, turn.
Row 3: 3 ch, 1 dc in ea of next 2 sts, *pc in next st, 1 dc in ea of next 3 sts, rep from * to end, turn.
Rep rows 2–3 for required length.

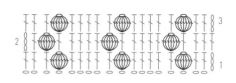

OFF-SET POPCORN COLUMNS

Note: This design uses 7-dc popcorns. Change color along each row to work the popcorns in a contrasting yarn.

Foundation: Make a multiple of 6 ch, plus 3.

Row 1: 1 dc in fourth ch from hook, 1 dc in next ch, *1 pc in next ch, 1 dc in ea of next 5 ch, rep from * to end, omitting 2 dc at end of final rep, turn.

Row 2: 3 ch, 1 dc in next st, *1 pc in next st, 1 dc in ea of next 5 sts, rep from * to end, omitting 1 dc at end of last rep, turn.

Row 3: 3 ch, 1 dc in ea of next 2 sts, *1 pc in next st, 1 dc in ea of next 5 sts, rep from * to end, omitting 2 dc at end of last rep, turn.

Rep rows 2–3 for required length. Fasten off.

PACKED POPCORNS

Note: This design uses a number of different dc in the popcorns—see supplementary chart for details. Change color along each row to work the popcorns in a contrast yarn.

Foundation: Make a multiple of 4 ch, plus 3 (the worked example used 23 ch).

Row 1: 1 dc in fourth ch from hook, *1 pc in next ch, 1 dc in ea of next 3 ch, rep from * to end, omitting 1 dc at end of last rep turn.

Row 2: 3 ch, 1 dc in next st, *1 pc in next pc, 1 dc in ea of next 3 dc, rep from * to end, omitting 1 dc at end of last rep turn.

Rows 3–6: Rep row 2, changing numbers of dc in ea pc as stated in the second chart.

The supplementary chart (below) indicates the number of dc to be used in each popcorn.

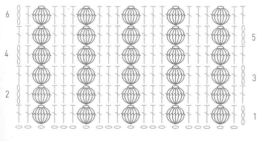

13	3	13	3	13
11	5	11	5	11
9	7	9	7	9
7	9	7	9	7
5	11	5	11	5
3	13	3	13	3

Chain Stitch

Chain stitch provides many exciting opportunities to create unusual textured effects. The designs on these pages will help you to start exploring these possibilities.

ALIGNED CHAIN SPOTS

Foundation: Make a multiple of 3 ch.
Row 1: 1 sc in second ch from hook, 1 sc in ea ch to end, turn.
Row 2: 1 ch, 1 sc in ea of next 2 sts, *3 ch, 1 sc in ea of next 3 sts, rep from * to end, turn.
Row 3: 1 ch, 1 sc in ea sc to end, turn.
Rep rows 2–3 for required length.

CHAIN LOOPS (1)

Foundation: Make an odd number of ch.
Row 1: 1 sc in second ch from hook, *5 ch, 1 sc in ea of next 2 foundation ch, rep from * to end, omitting 1 ch at end of last rep, turn.
Row 2: 1 ch, 1 sc in next st, *5 ch, 1 sc in ea of next 2 sc in prev row, rep from * to end.
Rep row 2 for required length. Work 1 row sc.

chain

+
single crochet

CHAIN LOOPS (2)

Note: Loops at left of sample are allowed to remain free. Loops at right of sample are interlinked vertically.
Foundation: Make a multiple of 3 ch.
Row 1: 1 sc in second ch from hook, 1 sc in ea ch to end, turn.

Row 2: 1 ch, 1 sc in ea of next 2 sts, *5 ch, 1 sc in ea of next 3 sts, rep from * to end, turn.
Row 3: 1 ch, 1 sc in ea sc to end, turn.
Rep rows 2-3 for required length. Interlink chain loops as described above.

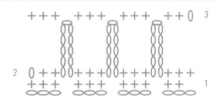

CHAIN SAMPLER

Note: Loops at left of sample should be interlinked from left to right to produce a plaited effect. Loops in the middle of the sample should be interlinked vertically. Loops at right of sample should be interlinked horizontally and then vertically, as shown in the supplementary diagram.
Foundation: Make 21 ch.
Row 1: 1 sc in second ch from hook, 1 sc in ea ch to end, turn.

Row 2: 1 ch, 1 sc in ea of next 2 sts, *11 ch, 1 sc in ea of next 3 sts, rep from * to end, turn. Change color.
Row 3: 1 ch, 1 sc in ea sc to end, turn.
Rep rows 2-3 to required length. Interlink chain loops as described above. Work one row of sc, including 1 sl st in top loop of interlinked chains.

Supplementary diagram

Puff Stitch

Puff stitches are useful additions to a crocheter's texture palette. Different densities can be achieved by using different numbers of yarn overs to form the stitch.

SMALL PUFFS

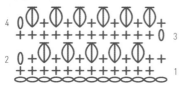

Note: In this stitch pattern, use 3 yo in each puff.
Foundation: Make an odd number of ch.
Row 1: 1 sc in second ch from hook, 1 sc in ea ch to end, turn.
Row 2: 1 ch, *1 sc, 1 puff, rep from * to last 2 sts, 2 sc, turn.
Row 3: 1 ch, 1 sc in ea st to end, turn.
Row 4: 1 ch, *1 puff, 1 sc, rep from * to end, turn.
Row 5: Rep row 3.
Rep rows 2–5 for required length, ending with an sc row.

JUST PUFFS

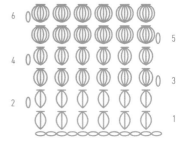

Note: Rows 1–2 use 3 yo in each puff, rows 3–4 use 5 yo in each puff, rows 5–6 use 7 yo in each puff. This design would make a lovely cuff.
Foundation: Make an even number of ch.
Row 1: 1 puff in second ch from hook, *skip 1 ch, 1 puff in next ch, rep from * to last end, turn.
Row 2: 1 ch, 1 puff in ea puff to end, turn.
Rows 3–6: Rep row 2, using the stated number of yo in ea puff.

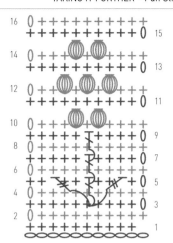

O
chain

+
single crochet

SPECIAL STITCHES

front post double/ treble

puff stitch (number of lines indicates number of yarn overs)

PUFF STITCH FLOWER PANEL

Note: The puff stitch in this design uses 5 yo.
Foundation: Make 11 ch.
Row 1: 1 sc in second ch from hook, 1 sc in ea ch to end, turn.
Row 2: 1 ch, 1 sc in ea st to end, turn.
Rows 3–4: Rep row 2.
Row 5: 1 ch, 1 sc, 1 FPtr around center st of row 3, 2 sc, 1 FPdc around center st of row 3, 2 sc, 1 FPtr around same st as last FPtr, 2 sc, turn.
Row 6: Rep row 2.

Row 7: 1 ch, 4 sc, 1 FPdc around FPdc in center st of row 5, 5 sc, turn.
Row 8: Rep row 2.
Row 9: Rep row 7.
Row 10: 1 ch, 3 sc, 1 puff, 1 sc, 1 puff, 4 sc, turn.
Row 11: Rep row 2.
Row 12: 1 ch, 2 sc, 1 puff, 1 sc, 1 puff, 1 sc, 1 puff, 3 sc, turn.
Row 13: Rep row 2.
Row 14: Rep row 10.
Rows 15–16: Rep row 2. Fasten off.

Clusters

Clusters can be worked over a number of stitches. In this selection, a number of stitches are worked (to the last yarn over) in a single stitch and with the final yarn over, a single top loop is created for the cluster. They show up best on the wrong side of the row they are worked on.

ALIGNED CLUSTERS

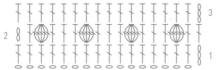

Foundation: Make a multiple of 4 ch, plus 3.
Row 1: 1 dc in fourth ch from hook, 1 dc in ea ch to end, turn.
Row 2: 3 ch, 1 dc, *5-dc cluster in next st, 3 dc, rep from * to end, omitting 1 dc from end of final rep, turn.
Row 3: 3 ch, 1 dc in ea st to end, turn.
Rep rows 2–3 for required length.

REVERSIBLE CLUSTERS

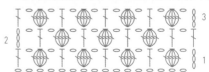

Foundation: Make a multiple of 4 ch.
Row 1: 5 dc cluster in sixth ch from hook, 1 ch, skip next ch, 1 dc in next ch, 1 ch, skip next ch, *5-dc cluster in next ch, 1 ch, skip next ch, 1 dc in next ch, 1 ch, skip next ch, rep from * to last 2 ch, 1 ch, skip next ch, 1 dc in next ch, turn.
Row 2: 4 ch, *1 dc in next cluster, 1 ch, 5-dc cluster in next dc, 1 ch, rep from * to last cluster, 1 ch, 1 dc in third of turning ch, turn.
Row 3: 4 ch, *5-dc cluster in next dc, 1 ch, 1 dc in next cluster, 1 ch, rep from * to end, omitting 1 ch from end of last rep, turn.
Rep rows 2–3 for required length.

SPACED-OUT REVERSIBLE CLUSTERS

Foundation: Make a multiple of 4 ch, plus 3.

Row 1: 1 dc in fourth ch from hook, *5-dc cluster in next st, 3 dc, rep from * to end omitting 1 dc from end of last rep, turn.

Row 2: 3 ch, 3 dc, *5-dc cluster in next st, 3 dc, rep from * to last st, 1 dc, turn.

Row 3: 3 ch, 1 dc, *5-dc cluster in next st, 3 dc, rep from * to end omitting 1 dc from end of last rep, turn.

Rep rows 2–3 for required length.

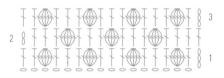

CLOSE CLUSTERS

Foundation: Make a multiple of 4 ch, plus 1.

Row 1: 1 sc in second ch from hook, 1 sc in ea ch to end, turn.

Row 2: 1 ch, 1 sc, *1 5-dc cluster in next st, 3 sc, rep from * to end omitting 1 sc from end of final rep, turn.

Row 3: 1 ch, 1 sc in ea st to end, turn.

Row 4: 1 ch, 3 sc, *1 5-dc cluster in next st, 3 sc, rep from * to last st, 1 sc, turn.

Row 5: Rep row 3.

Rep rows 2–5 for required length.

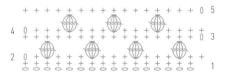

STITCH KEY

chain

single crochet

double crochet

SPECIAL STITCHES

5-dc cluster

SURFACE CROCHET

Surface crochet is worked into an existing item or fabric. There are two types of surface crochet—Tambour Style and Free Style.

Tambour Style

The yarn supply is held below the fabric. Slip stitch is thus the only possible stitch—the effect is like chain stitch embroidery. It can be used on its own, or in combination with other techniques.

TAMBOUR STYLE (1)

In this circle of hdc, one, two, or three strands are used (with different-sized hooks) to make a chain stitch over each stitch on an individual round.

TAMBOUR STYLE (2)

On this rectangle of dc, chain stitches are made over each dc across a row. As the rows are relatively tall, an additional chain is made—alternatively you could just elongate the stitches to match the height of the row instead.

TAMBOUR STYLE (3)

There is no reason why you have to be restricted by the grid formed by the stitches of the base fabric.

Free Style

The yarn is held above the base fabric, so you can use any crochet stitch you like.

FREE STYLE (1)

In this design, three dc are worked on each side of a filet mesh, with color changes to produce a rainbow ripple effect. The top left section differs from the lower right simply by working a sl st between the groups as you work along the chevron row.

To work the mesh fabric:

Foundation: make 17 ch.

Row 1: 1 dc in 6th ch from hook, * 1 ch, skip 1 ch, 1 dc in next ch, rep from * to end, turn.

Row 2: 4 ch, 1 dc in next dc, * 1 ch, 1 dc in next dc, rep from * to end, turn.

Rows 3–5: Rep row 2. Fasten off.

STITCH KEY

chain

double crochet

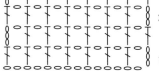

Start here

Filet mesh chart

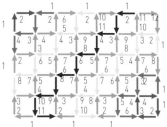

Color direction and order of work

FREE STYLE (2)

Work as for Filet mesh chart, above. Three dc are worked along the sides of the innermost block of stitches, three hdc in the middle block, and three sc on the outermost edges.

More Free Style Surface Crochet

You can experiment with surface crochet and work all kinds of pictures and patterns.

CHEVRONS

Shaped fabrics can have their unique features emphasized by the careful addition of simple surface stitches. In this design, dc is worked along the tops of alternate rows, with a 5-ch picot at the lowest points.

CRAB STITCH RAINBOW STRIPES

Chain-look hdc provides a textured surface that can be worked on without actually working right through the fabric. In this design, a row of crab stitch is worked along each of the chain effect rows.

ONE, TWO, THREE

In this design, different numbers of different stitches are worked along the tops of alternate rows, followed by a row of crab stitch in a contrasting color. In a play on words, one sc is worked in every stitch, two dc are worked in alternate stitches, and three tr are worked in every third stitch.

FOLIAGE

This sample shows that the placement of stitches need not be constrained by the grid structure of the base fabric. The lime green dc fans are worked into the fabric at different angles. The leaf green includes a puff stitch, a cluster, and a popcorn, with sc and chains to spread out these elements. The dark green includes a chain loop, a curlicue, and a repeat of one sc and one tr. The result looks somewhat like foliage.

FLOWER

Almost any of the other textured fabrics you produce from this book can be further enhanced with surface work, and any shape can be given surface embellishment. This design includes 5 dc popcorns, tambour-style chains, and 5 post-stitch fans.

TREE PICTURE

This design combines a tambour-style tree trunk and free style foliage formed from (left to right) crab stitch, puff stitches, dc fans, and chain loops anchored into the base fabric with sl st or sc.

Abbreviations and Symbols

These are the abbreviations and symbols used in this book.

Stitch	Abbreviation	Symbol	Stitch	Abbreviation	Symbol
Stitch(es)	st(s)	(none)	Wrap yarn over hook	yo	(none)
Chain	ch	o	Slip stitch in front loop only	(none)	○
Slip stitch	sl st	⌒	Slip stitch in middle loop only	(none)	⌒
Single crochet	sc	+	Slip stitch in back loop only	(none)	⌢
Half double crochet	hdc	T	Crab stitch	cr st	⌁
Double crochet	dc	⊤	Crab stitch in front loop only	(none)	⌁
Treble crochet	tr	⊤	Single crochet in front loop only	(none)	⌁
Double treble crochet	dtr	⊤	Single crochet in back loop only	(none)	⌁
Each	ea	(none)	Front post crab stitch	FPcr st	⌁
Loop	lp	(none)			
Repeat	rep	(none)			
Together	tog	(none)			
Space(s)	sp(s)	(none)	Single crochet in middle loop only	(none)	±
Turning chain	tch	(none)			

Stitch	Abbreviation	Symbol	Stitch	Abbreviation	Symbol
Front post single crochet	FPsc		Double crochet in back loop only	(none)	
Back post single crochet	BPsc		Double crochet in middle loop only	(none)	
Half double in front loop only	(none)		Front post double crochet	FPdc	
Half double in back loop only	(none)		Back post double crochet	BPdc	
Half double in middle loop only	(none)		Extended treble crochet	etr	
Front post half double crochet	FPhdc		Treble crochet in front loop only	(none)	
Back post half double crochet	BPhdc		Treble crochet in back loop only	(none)	
Extended double crochet	edc		Treble crochet in middle loop only	(none)	
Double crochet in front loop only	(none)		Front post treble crochet	FPtr	

Stitch	Abbreviation	Symbol	Stitch	Abbreviation	Symbol
Back post treble crochet	BPtr		Front post quintuple treble crochet	Fpquintr	
Double treble crochet in front loop only	(none)		Back post quintuple treble crochet	Bpquintr	
Double treble crochet in back loop only	(none)		Popcorn (using 3 dc)	pc	
Front post double treble crochet	FPdtr		Puff stitch (using 3 yo)	puff	
Back post double treble crochet	BPdtr		Front post puff stitch	FPpuff	
Front post triple treble crochet	FPttr		Cluster or bobble (using 3 dc)	(none)	
Back post triple treble crochet	BPttr		Front post cluster or bobble	(none)	
Front post quadruple treble crochet	FPquadtr				
Back post quadruple treble crochet	BPquadtr				

At-a-glance: Basic Abbreviations and Symbols

Leave this flap open as you work though the book for an instant reference to the basic stitches, abbreviations, and symbols.

Index